just plain smart ™

tax planning
advisor

A year-round
approach to lowering
your taxes this year,
next year and beyond

**RANDOM HOUSE
REFERENCE**

just plain smart ™

tax
planning
advisor

H&R BLOCK

table of contents with selected topics

introduction

Is income tax one of your favorite subjects? Probably not. But what if by learning about taxes you could keep more of your hard-earned money?

Many Americans ignore their taxes until April and miss extraordinary opportunities to save. Why? Maybe it's because they don't realize that they can reduce what they pay in taxes, or even get back some of the money they have already paid. Or maybe it's because tax laws are complicated. Complying with all of the requirements takes a lot of time and effort. It's easier to put off thinking about taxes until tax time, especially when there may be better things to do. But if you want to get serious about tax-saving, you need to plan ahead.

The **H&R Block Tax Planning Advisor** introduces you to a year-round approach to tax planning that can help simplify things a bit. Year-round doesn't mean that you'll have to think about taxes each and every day of the year. Instead, it means that by knowing more about taxes you'll be prepared for tax-saving opportunities as they present themselves. Whenever possible, you can plan ahead to help reduce your tax liability. We think this approach is just plain smart.

The **Tax Planning Advisor** is the first book in the H&R Block just plain smart Advisor Series of helpful and reliable tax and financial guides. As the world's largest tax services company, H&R Block has the experience to understand your financial goals and knows how to help you achieve them. Use the H&R Block just plain smart Advisor Series to put our experience to work for you.

How To Use This Book

The **Tax Planning Advisor** is designed for those who want to exercise more control over their taxes and personal finances. It covers a wide variety of tax planning information, from what documents to keep to the details on deductions, exemptions, and credits. The book features dozens of sidebars—useful "fast facts," action-packed "smart steps," and clear "plain talk" definitions. It also contains scenarios derived from real-life tax situations. This guide should arm you with the knowledge you need to plan ahead, reduce your taxes, and keep more money in your pocket.

Ideally, you should read the **Tax Planning Advisor** from cover to cover. We've organized it as a step-by-step approach. If you have time to do everything at once, that's great. If you're like most people and are pressed for time, then implement what you can, set the book aside, and pick it up later. You'll also want to keep it handy throughout the year as certain events occur (like getting married or having a baby). You can make adjustments as your personal situation changes.

What's the Next Step?

Decide how much of the **Tax Planning Advisor** is applicable to you and choose what steps to take. Keep the book around for future use. Use it to make or modify your plans and to ask informed questions of your professional advisors. Whether you want to do it all on your own or let someone help you out, you'll be better equipped to pay only your fair share of taxes—and not a penny more.

H&R Block

Acknowledgments

While it is not possible to list everyone who made the **H&R Block Tax Planning Advisor** possible, we would like to acknowledge the following organizations and individuals for their many contributions to this book: **The College for Financial Planning** ■ **Practice Development Institute, Inc.** ■ **Random House Reference** ■ **RSM McGladrey** ■ **and the many dedicated associates and tax professionals of H&R Block.**

1 [TAXES 101:
An Introduction to Taxes]

"The Congress shall have power to lay and collect
taxes on incomes, from whatever source derived,
without apportionment among the several States,
and without regard to any census or enumeration."
—Sixteenth Amendment
to the U.S. Constitution

Former U.S. Supreme Court Justice Oliver Wendell Holmes, Jr. once said, "taxes are what we pay for civilized society."

Holmes was on to something. After all, how could society exist without **taxes**? The U.S. Constitution contains passages that describe the need to establish a more perfect union, secure a common defense, and promote the general welfare. Doing big things like that takes money. So every tax season, we, the people, gather our check stubs, bank statements, and W-2 forms, and visit our tax professionals. Then we contribute to Uncle Sam the money it takes to run this great country.

Where does all of our hard-earned money go? It pays for a full menu of social needs, including police officers; fire departments; our military and homeland defense; Social Security; health care; our justice system; highways; safety of our food and water; and libraries. Then there's welfare and care for the needy and the poor, foreign aid assistance for other countries, and programs that help the disabled. Taxes also pay for the educational system that teaches our young and gives them dreams for an exciting future, and disaster relief for those that have endured floods, hurricanes, or tornados.

The way we spend our money for social causes, via our taxes, says a lot about our country and people. But there are legal reasons for paying your taxes as well. The Sixteenth Amendment to the U.S. Constitution gives Congress the power to collect income taxes. Congress, in turn, has empowered the Internal Revenue Service to fulfill those tax-collecting duties. Hefty fines and possibly a stretch in one of our other tax-funded entities—the U.S. prison system—await those who evade paying their fair share of taxes.

Generally speaking, you can't live in the United States of America, the greatest country of all, without paying taxes. While none of us likes to give up his or her hard-earned money, most of us value the benefits that come as a result of paying taxes.

A Brief History of Taxes

Taxes have been with us forever. Well, at least since the dawn of civilization. Egyptian pharaohs sent scribes into the countryside to collect taxes on land, cooking oil, livestock, and beer. In ancient Greece, citizens paid a special tax called the *eisphora* to fund the military during times of war. During the Roman Empire, working Romans were required to pay tax collectors a portion of their earnings to build state-of-the-art sewers, aqueducts, arenas, roads, and coliseums.

Fast-forward 1,500 or more years to the dawn of American civilization, and you can see that taxes played just as big a role in the development of our country. In the colonies, the British regulated trade and required colonists to pay taxes on items like sugar and indigo. The British also levied heavy customs taxes on colonial exports, especially tobacco from Virginia, and the king's coffers swelled.

In 1763, England emerged victorious from the Seven Years War, during which it gained overwhelming control of the seas and shipping trade. To pay military bills and other expenses in its growing empire, the British enforced greater excise (sales) taxes on the colonies. In 1765, the English Parliament passed the Stamp Act, which required colonists to buy stamps for printed materials such as legal documents, newspapers, and land titles. Benjamin Franklin and others were outraged by this new type of tax and demanded that, in return, the colonies be represented in Parliament. "No taxation without representation," they said.

Led by Franklin and others, the resistance to English taxes and governance grew. In 1773, a tax on tea led irate patriots to dump approximately 350 crates of tea into Boston Harbor. That mayhem helped trigger the Revolutionary War, which brought about America's freedom.

One of the first things our Founding Fathers found after the Revolutionary War was a huge bill from the overseas allies who had helped finance the battle. In 1787, figuring that an income tax on the heels of a war against taxation wouldn't fly, the young government decided to place levies only on consumer items such as tobacco, liquor, and sugar.

That strategy worked fairly well for eighty-odd years, until the onset of the Civil War. During that war, both the North and South needed money for military expenses, but only the North succeeded in raising as much as 21 percent of it through taxes. In 1861, Congress introduced the first income tax, which levied 3 percent on annual incomes over $800, an amount that exempted most families even after it was later dropped to $600.

The Internal Revenue Service (IRS)

The IRS dates from 1862, at the beginning of the Civil War, when President Lincoln approved legislation creating a Bureau of Internal Revenue. The agency has a simple mission: to collect our taxes. The IRS enforces the tax laws passed by Congress.

Every year the IRS assists millions of taxpayers with filing their returns. These people call the toll-free IRS tax hotline, search through thousands of Web pages at www.irs.gov, send letters requesting help, or visit one of the many IRS field offices.

In 1996, mounting complaints about the process of collecting taxes led Congress to set up a commission to reform the IRS. The commission's report led to a 1998 tax law that greatly expanded taxpayers' rights and established a Taxpayer Advocate Service as an independent voice inside the agency. The IRS is endeavoring to become more taxpayer-friendly. Nonetheless, it's smart to know your rights as a taxpayer. See Chapter 11 for more information.

Types of Taxes

Various government agencies collect an assortment of taxes, including:

Excise Taxes—These taxes (like the luxury tax) are collected on the manufacture, sale, and consumption of specified commodities.

Federal Estate Tax—Sometimes called the "death tax," this tax is levied when property is transferred from the deceased to his or her heirs, legatees, or devisees.

Federal Gift Tax—This tax is levied on the donor of a gift and is based in part on the amount or value of the gift.

Franchise Tax—This tax is charged to businesses for the privilege of operating in a state or local jurisdiction.

Income Taxes—Taxes on salaries, wages, tips, and commissions, as well as other income sources such as dividends and interest from savings accounts. Both individuals and corporations are subject to income taxes.

fast fact

Taxes you pay on real estate and personal property are deductible as itemized deductions on your federal income tax return.

fast fact

The earliest income tax in the U.S. appeared in New England in 1643. The New Plymouth Colony levied a faculties tax—a poll tax with graduated rates—which is the simplest form of income tax.

Personal Property Tax—A tax levied annually and based on the value of certain personal property such as automobiles and boats.

Real Property Tax—This is based on the value of realty (such as land and buildings) owned by nonexempt individuals or organizations.

Sales Tax—Gross receipts from the retail sale of tangible personal property (such as clothes, automobiles, and equipment) and certain services form the basis of this tax.

Social Security and Medicare Tax—Also called the Federal Insurance Contribution Act (FICA), this tax is a payment shared by employee and employer. The proceeds from this tax provide Social Security and Medicare benefits to those eligible.

Unemployment Tax—The Federal Unemployment Tax Act (FUTA) is charged only to employers. Various states receive FUTA funds for their unemployment benefit programs.

The Ever-Changing Tax Scene

While government agencies continue to collect taxes in one way or another, it's smart to keep up with the ever-changing tax laws. Understanding how the changes affect you will play a big part in determining how much you are able to reduce your tax liability. Here are a few of the areas where the tax law has recently changed. We'll cover these in more detail later on.

- **You can adopt a child and have the government pay more of your costs.**
- **You can contribute more to your tax-favored retirement plan.**
- **You can take a new deduction for higher education expenses.**
- **You have improved options for saving for education expenses.**
- **You may be able to resume deducting student loan interest.**

[THE CHALLENGE]

Scott, a bachelor in his forties, was sometimes disappointed with his check on payday. When he looked at his pay stub it was full of deductions for things like health insurance and taxes. Although he had money withheld for income taxes, he still had to write a check every April to finish paying what he owed. To make matters worse, Scott had just purchased a house and didn't have any extra money to save for retirement. It seemed as if everyone was taking a bite out of Scott's income, and there wasn't much left over.

THE PLAN

When it came time to prepare and file his income tax return, Scott gathered up his checkbook and tax records for a visit with his tax professional. After the tax professional reviewed Scott's documents, he asked Scott about putting some money aside in an Individual Retirement Arrangement (IRA). "Sure, all I need to do is win the lottery to come up with the money," Scott replied. "How can I afford to invest in an IRA when I still have a check to write to Uncle Sam?" Scott's tax professional explained that he didn't owe any money this year. Instead, he was due a sizable refund that could be used toward his retirement. Scott wondered how this could have happened.

The tax professional explained that Scott was due a refund because he purchased a home earlier in the year and did not adjust his withholding accordingly. He was having more money than necessary withheld from his paycheck. The refund could be used toward his retirement savings. "Well, maybe I didn't win the lottery, but it feels like it to me!" Scott exclaimed. "I'm glad I have the money for my IRA now, but I'd rather have it in each of my paychecks instead of at the end of the year. Next time I do something big, I'm going to get tax advice right away so I can have access to as much of my money as possible."

Impact on Americans

No family reunion passes without Uncle Ted moaning about this year's tax bill. But most Americans pay their taxes every year without too much fuss, and they're often paying more than necessary. Taxes are often regarded as something over which most people have no control, like the weather or the stock market. They're something to gripe about, but nothing to do anything about.

Call it dread or denial, but this lack of aggressive and deliberate tax planning is costing taxpayers plenty. By failing to establish a tax-planning regimen, many Americans are denying themselves tens of thousands of dollars, if not more, over the course of their lives.

The General Accounting Office (GAO) reports that as many as 2.2 million people overpay their taxes annually because they claim the standard **deduction** instead of itemizing. The average overpayment to the IRS is $438. This may not seem like much, but $438 invested every year could yield a tidy sum. You could use that money toward a retirement or vacation home, or a small business when you retire.

Did You Know That. . . ?

To be a tax-wise citizen, you don't need to know every nook and cranny of the federal income tax code, but you do need to know some basics as they apply to your life. Here are a few things you might not have known about income taxes.

Did You Know That. . . ?

Setting up a record-keeping system that will ensure you don't miss a single deduction, exemption, or credit for which you're eligible is a fairly simple matter? See Chapter 2 for help with this most basic of tax-planning strategies.

You might not be required to file a federal income tax return? If your income is low enough, you might not meet the gross income filing requirement and can forget the whole business for this year at least. But, even if you're not *required* to file a return, you'll want to anyway if doing so nets you a refund. See Chapter 3 to determine if you're required to file.

If you withdrew money from a certificate of deposit early and paid a penalty for doing so, you may be eligible for a deduction even if you don't itemize? See Chapter 4 for a discussion of line 32, Form 1040.

You may be able to deduct expenses for programs to help you quit smoking, lose weight, or overcome alcohol or drug addiction? You can find out more in Chapter 5.

The amount of time you own a stock or other investment can have a dramatic effect on how much tax you'll pay when you sell? See the discussion on holding periods in Chapter 6.

You need to be careful about when you withdraw funds from an Individual Retirement Arrangement (IRA)? If you make the wrong move, a 10 percent or greater penalty may apply. Play it safe and learn more about tax-favored retirement plans of all kinds in Chapter 7.

Hiring your children to work in your business can have beneficial tax consequences? Chapter 8 will tell you how to make this tactic work for you.

There are numerous tax breaks to help you save for and pay college costs? These tax breaks include credits, deductions, and tax-favored savings accounts. All your options are spelled out in Chapter 9.

■ **If you owe more than you can currently pay when you file your return, you may be able to pay in installments?** And that's only one way out of this unfortunate situation. See Chapter 10.

■ **In the event your return is audited by the IRS, the law provides you with several important rights?** See Chapter 11 to learn about your rights and how to exercise them.

■ **Your computer can be one of your best tax friends?** With a computer and the Internet you can learn about the tax code, get help preparing your return, and even file electronically. See Chapter 12 to learn all about how your computer can help you with your year-round tax plan.

Take time to learn about the tax law. Use your knowledge to ask your tax professional the most constructive questions that can help reduce your tax liability. This will keep more of your hard-earned money in your pocket—and out of Uncle Sam's.

the ESSENTIALS

1 The Sixteenth Amendment of the U.S. Constitution was passed into law in 1913. It authorized Congress to levy income taxes on U.S. citizens to fund government operations.

2 Founded in 1862, the IRS's mission is to collect taxes and enforce tax laws enacted by Congress.

3 Taxpayers deny themselves tens of thousands of dollars, if not more, over the course of their lives if they fail to put an aggressive tax-planning campaign in place.

2 [RECORDS ARE MEANT TO BE KEPT: Developing a Record-Keeping System]

"A place for everything and everything in its place."
—English Proverb

Stay abreast of new developments to wring every possible deduction and credit out of a tax year. Keep good records and stay organized all year long.

The people who win at the tax game plan year-round. Unless you do a good job of planning and keeping records all year, there aren't many last-minute strategies to save you big money. If you aren't well prepared, chances are you'll finish your tax return in a flurry and rush to the post office at midnight. As a result, you could miss some important exemptions, deductions, and credits—and pay more tax than is required of you.

Why not avoid that anxiety? Take a big-picture approach to managing your taxes. Look upon it as a year-long marathon rather than a one-week sprint. Think of the April headaches you'll avoid, and even better, all the money you'll save.

Mark Your Calendar

A smart approach to organizing your tax-planning calendar is based on the seasons. **January**, **February**, and **March** are the perfect months to set up your tax strategy for the coming year and determine how you're going to keep records. In **April**, you will close the books on the previous year's tax return. That's also a perfect time to review how well you did at keeping records last year and how you could do better.

Now, with a good record-keeping plan, **May**, **June**, **July**, and **August** are the months for paying attention to your tax professional's suggestions for an even less painful April next tax season. This might be a good time to change your withholding if it was too much or too little last year. But it is also important to stay on top of your record keeping. If you forget your taxes, your records soon turn sloppy and incomplete, undermining your good intentions to make the tax law work for you.

In early **November**, open your computer spreadsheet, or grab some paper and a calculator. Review pay stubs or income records and determine how much you've earned so far this year. Then estimate how much you'll make the remaining two months. Now that you have an estimated figure of total income for the year, you can start cutting your tax liability with exemptions, deductions, and credits. Use last year's tax return to guide you, along with the advice from your tax professional. Double-check your records for any new items not on last year's return. When you finish this exercise, you should have an estimated taxable income figure. From this you can quickly see how smart and legal tax maneuvers will save you money. If you are in the 27 percent bracket, for example, every $1,000 you shave off your taxable income figure reduces your tax bill by about $270.

December is the time to make final decisions before the year-end tax deadlines, including how much money to stash in your 401(k), whether to make additional charitable contributions, or whether you should take capital losses on any poorly performing investments (there's much more on taxes and investing in Chapter 6). As the month winds down, finish your year-end financial paperwork so you'll be ready when it's time to file your tax return and be rewarded for the consistent planning you've done all year. As you usher the old year out and ring the new year in, it is time to start the process all over again.

Remember why you're going through this trouble. Buried deep within the vast ocean of tax law is a virtual treasure trove of tax-saving opportunities. Every dollar counts, whether you're managing gains and losses from stock sales, taking a depreciation deduction on business equipment, or making a year-end charitable contribution (Uncle Sam rewards you for helping worthy causes). As many people have learned, regularly reviewing your tax situation may be the smartest financial move you'll ever make.

Bad record
keeping usually
leads to painful
audit results.
Without clear
documentation,
the IRS can dis-
allow unproven
deductions and
credits, which
can lead to
penalties and
interest in addi-
tion to more
taxes being
due.

Should You Hire a Tax Professional?

Having a trusted tax professional is highly advisable. (We admit it: we're biased.) This is especially true if your income is growing, or if you've begun a family, bought a home, made some investments, run a home-based or small business, or just can't keep up with the constantly changing tax laws. While you focus your time and attention on experiencing the joys and challenges of these life events, a tax professional keeps an eye on your purse strings to make sure you don't pay any more tax than is required.

Good tax professionals don't just add and subtract your numbers and fill out tax forms. They ask and answer key tax questions and help you find legal deductions and credits that you might not be aware existed. Your tax professional can also be a year-round advisor. For example, what are the tax consequences of with-drawing funds from your IRA? Should you close on your new home in December or wait until January? Choices you make have significant tax implications.

Every year, people who once prepared their own tax returns turn to trusted tax professionals for valuable assistance. Many others who want to do their own tax preparation are seeking advice and sometimes asking a tax professional to review their final returns. The tax code is so complicated that many taxpayers turn to knowledgeable professionals for the peace of mind that their returns are done right and that they have reduced their tax liability as much as possible.

Records = Taxes Saved

Whether or not you hire a professional, tax preparation can become confusing if your records aren't straight. Some items require detailed tax records to give you the biggest possible benefit, such as mortgage and investment interest deductions, unreimbursed employee business expenses, and charitable contributions. If you can't document these things come tax time, you'll miss a golden opportunity.

Think of all the paperwork, filing, and bookkeeping as little jobs that pay you money when tax season rolls around. This will make the tasks feel less like chores. Tracking details like receipts from your business lunches will save you money. Be sure to write on the receipt the names of everyone at the lunch and the business topic you covered, then file those receipts together in the same folder as the year passes. You'll quickly realize how a solid record-keeping system is the foundation for a solid tax plan.

Throwing all your records in a shoebox under the bed can lead to disaster. Sloppy filing can make your records so haphazard that you can't readily document your expenses, which could lead not only to missed deductions, but also to a particularly painful experience if you're audited. Too many of us look upon keeping good records as a burden instead of a benefit. The IRS accepts the word of the overwhelming majority every year when millions of tax returns are filed. But if the IRS questions your return, the law places the burden of proof on you, the taxpayer. As a result, it is essential that you maintain accurate records in case the IRS selects your return for an audit.

What types of things should you keep in your files? Obviously, you should be able to verify the income, expenses, exemptions, deductions, payments, and credits you report on your return. Generally speaking, you need these same documents—check stubs, old tax returns, receipts, and the like—to manage your business and track your personal finances.

Make Your System Work for You

There is no cookie-cutter way to organize your tax records. You must set up a system that works for you. Get advice from friends, neighbors, and relatives if you like, but build a filing system that fits your way of finding things. Why such an open-ended approach? Because finding documents when you need them is the real test of whether your system works for you. Here's a

smart step

People organize things in different ways. Make sure your record-keeping system makes sense to *you*.

good rule of thumb: Organize your records in such a way that you can open a file drawer and find a document in less than five minutes every time, without fail. To reach this goal, keep your system simple and keep it current.

Some people like to use a stack of plain manila folders. You can write the main categories on labels, sort them alphabetically, and stick them in the file drawer.

Others prefer to do everything electronically, downloading banking and financial management software off the Internet or purchasing it at a store. You might find spreadsheet software an easy way to get things organized. Or you might prefer applications that record your income and expenses and keep track of your checking and savings accounts, especially if you use online banking and bill payment. Just be sure to back up your financial data so you don't inadvertently lose all that rich information when you need it most. Remember, too, that we live in an age when computers need to be checked for viruses. A malicious bug can rip through your hard drive in a nanosecond and mangle the contents before you can say, "I'm being audited."

If the high-tech approach doesn't suit you, a basic filing cabinet or desk drawer will do just fine. Just make sure that same drawer doesn't become a cluttered mess over time, potentially mixing up your files and discouraging you from keeping it orderly. You might want to keep your tax files separate from other documents. For example, if your golf scorecards end up in the same file folder with your daughter's student loan payments, you could worsen your handicap in more ways than one.

The first step in record keeping is to acquire:

- **A filing cabinet or desk drawer to store your records**
- **File folders**
- **Labels to tag the folders**
- **A pen or marker**

  and/or

- **A reliable computer, your favorite financial spreadsheet or software, and disks for making back-ups of your files for electronic record keeping.**

What Tax-Related Records to Keep

Since receipts can pile up over time, you may be relieved to hear that you don't have to keep a file for every penny spent (although some people do just that by using their computer software). Clearly, some records stand out as keepers. Here's a snapshot of what you should hang on to:

Charitable Giving Information—Keep receipts for all your contributions. If a contribution exceeds $75 and is partly for goods and services, you must obtain a statement from the charity providing a good-faith estimate of the value. To deduct donations of $250 or more made at any one time, you must have written confirmation from the recipient organization. Keep a log of out-of-pocket expenses for charitable work, such as bus and taxi fares, auto mileage, tolls, parking fees, and the cost and cleaning of uniforms. In your records, enter the name of the charity, the date of the expenses, and the amount.

Gambling Records—This can be a simple log that lists the type of gambling activity, how much money you won or lost, the location or address of the estab-

smart step

Take photographs of valuable property for substantiation in case of theft or damage. Be sure to store them in a secure location such as a safe deposit box.

lishment, the date, and the names of others who were present with you, if applicable. Also be sure to keep any Forms W-2G you receive. These are especially valuable because they will show any taxes withheld from your winnings.

General Financial Documents—Keep documents such as pay stubs, W-2 forms, records of tips you were paid, sales receipts or contracts for big-ticket items such as the purchase or sale of an automobile (if used for business) or home, investment records, along with contributions to retirement accounts, bank and brokerage statements, Form 1099, and mortgage interest statements.

Insurance and Medical Records—Save all papers regarding insurance claims and medical expenses, including medical insurance if it is not subsidized by an employer, along with dates and specifics as to what was paid for, when it was paid, and what was reimbursed by insurance (if applicable).

Receipts for Deductible Items—If you pay for deductible items using a credit card, electronic funds transfer, or personal check, make sure you record the check number (or keep your credit card and/or bank statements), dollar amount, payee's name, and date of the transaction. If you make a payment in cash, you will need to get a dated receipt showing the amount. On the back of the receipt, write the reason the expense is deductible.

Self-Employment Records—People who are self-employed or use their homes for business need to keep a special set of records. We recommend that you contact your tax professional for advice and additional information. There's much more on tax and small business issues in Chapter 8.

Theft or Loss Documentation—If you suffered a theft or casualty loss, document it by including the property's value before and after the theft or casualty, the date the property was first noticed missing or damaged, and proof that it was yours. It might be necessary to have a copy of the police report, if one was filed, especially if the item was very valuable.

Some folks like to separate their tax records into current and long-term files. You probably will want to implement some form of this idea. Current tax files should include all of the items mentioned above for the current tax year (for example, if you received a bonus check from your employer in the first quarter, keep it in your current general finance file). Long-term files should contain at least six years of tax returns (more on that later) and relevant supporting documents. The same goes for home improvement receipts and relevant canceled checks.

If you operate a home-based or other small business, be sure to maintain separate files for your personal records and your business records. This will make it easier for you to know which deductions and credits you're entitled to as a business owner and which you're entitled to on the personal portion of your return. Keeping separate sets of records prevents accidental duplication and potentially confusing overlap of what goes where.

As we mentioned earlier, a variety of software programs on the market are specifically designed to help you maintain good tax records. Even if you use software, hold onto physical receipts and tax forms to support your electronic records. If the IRS wants to check your records, they will most likely ask to see original receipts and tax forms. It's a good idea to file your information from each tax year in a folder, large envelope, or binder. You can store these yearly files in boxes or on shelves in case you need them.

Above all, always file your tax records in order by date, organized by category. Keeping up with your receipts, pay stubs, and various financial forms as the year goes along will make it easier to find the numbers you need at tax time.

smart step

If you keep track of your tax records electronically, be sure to keep original paper receipts and documents.

Records Checklist

For tax purposes, there are many records you'll want to keep, so use this checklist as you create your files. Your personal list may not include all of these and may include others.

✓ ───▶ **Income**

- [ ] **Alimony received** (divorce decree and ex-spouse's Social Security number)
- [ ] **Capital gains and losses** (records of date acquired, cost and selling price, and Forms 1099-B)
- [ ] **Distributions from IRAs** (all forms, such as Forms 1099-R and 8606 showing nondeductible contributions, until the account is closed)
- [ ] **Distributions from other retirement plans** (Forms 1099-R and employer-supplied documents, pensions, annuities, and insurance contracts)
- [ ] **Employment earnings and tips received** (W-2 forms and records of tips received)
- [ ] **Gains from the sale of business-use property**
- [ ] **Interest and dividends received** (Forms 1099-INT, 1099-OID, and 1099-DIV)
- [ ] **Miscellaneous income** (gambling winnings/losses, prizes, jury duty fees, income from your hobby)
- [ ] **Nontaxable income and gifts** (municipal bond interest, receipts for nontaxable items, records of the donor's basis, proof of fair market value at date gift was received, and any gift tax paid)
- [ ] **Partnerships, S corporations** (Schedules K-1 and all records of investment)
- [ ] **Real estate rental income** (lease agreements, closing statements, contracts, documents reflecting repairs and improvements made, rent and security deposits received, and breakdown of depreciation from previous tax years)
- [ ] **Self-employment records** (invoices, receipts, and Forms 1099)
- [ ] **Social Security and Railroad Retirement benefits** (Forms SSA-1099, RRB-1099, and RRB-1099-R)

☐ **State and local income tax refunds** (Form 1099-G)
☐ **Unemployment compensation** (Form 1099-G)

✓ ───► **Expenses**

☐ **Adoption expenses** (legal fees, adoption fees, court costs, travel costs, and other costs directly related to adopting a child)

☐ **Alimony payments** (divorce decree, your ex-spouse's Social Security number, and canceled checks showing your payments)

☐ **Casualty/theft losses** (police and insurance reports, receipts for the items and/or any documentation to help demonstrate their fair market value before and after the property was destroyed, damaged, or stolen)

☐ **Charitable contributions** (canceled checks, appraisals, receipts from the charity recording the amount and date of gift, and the value of items received in return, any out-of-pocket expenses, and mileage traveled while providing services to a charitable organization)

☐ **Child-care expenses** (amounts you pay either for the care of your children under age thirteen or for your spouse or dependents who are unable to care for themselves while you're at work)

☐ **Classroom supply receipts** (if you're an educator and have out-of-pocket expenses for classroom supplies)

☐ **Education expenses** (for yourself, your spouse, and your dependents)

☐ **Foreign income taxes paid** (income taxes you paid to a foreign government, usually shown on your year-end brokerage statement if paid as part of your investment portfolio)

☐ **Home mortgage and investment interest expenses** (Form 1098 all documents, including statements that outline the terms of a loan, notes, and canceled checks)

☐ **Medical/dental expenses** (copies of paid bills, insurance policies, canceled checks, receipts for payments, receipts for prescriptions, records for amounts deducted by employers for medical insurance, receipts of expenses for which you were reimbursed, and travel expenses including mileage)

smart step

Keep tax returns for at least six years before destroying them.

☐ **Retirement plan contributions** (statements showing contributions made and a copy of the plan)

☐ **Student loan interest paid** (canceled checks showing your payments and Form 1098-E)

☐ **Taxes paid** (prior-year state tax return if additional tax was paid along with correlating canceled check, W-2 forms for state income tax withheld, copies of checks for estimated state tax payments, and tax documents supporting deductions for any other deductible taxes paid, such as personal property tax)

☐ **Unreimbursed business expenses** (detailed diary of expenses, all business receipts, canceled checks, and credit card slips)

☐ **Wages paid to household employees** (wages paid and taxes remitted for employees such as house cleaners, gardeners, and child-care providers if the services were performed in your home)

What Can You Throw Away?

Hollywood studio chief Samuel Goldwyn was known for his rapier-like wit and funny plays on words. One day his secretary was cleaning out the office file cabinets. She asked him if she could toss files that were no longer necessary. "Sure," he said. "Just as long as you make copies of everything."

Goldwyn's idea is pretty good when it comes to tax records. You certainly don't want to throw away your financial records too soon. Then again, unless you're a pack rat and love to save fifteen-year-old water bills and gift receipts, you might want to make room for new records.

When it comes to discarding old records, the same rule of thumb applies as mentioned earlier: keep it simple and consistent. The IRS generally requires you to keep tax records three years from the date you file your return or the due date of your return if later. By law, the IRS has three years to question a return. If you underreport your gross income by more than 25 percent, they can go back six years. If they find outright fraud, they can go back as many years as they want.

Be conservative when tossing files. Hang on to your tax records for six years, especially important documents such as tax returns, pay stubs, and your checking account statements. In addition, it's a good idea to hang onto certain forms indefinitely. For example, the IRS recommends that you keep copies of your W-2 forms until you're eligible for retirement in case there's a discrepancy with the Social Security Administration records. The IRS eventually discards tax returns so you may want to hang on to your copies in case you or your family needs them if you're ill or if you pass away, or if you need to substantiate your earnings for retirement income or insurance purposes.

It doesn't hurt to hang on to copies of yearly individual retirement arrangement statements from your investment firm. Also keep copies of Form 8606 that you file with your return. This form documents your basis in your traditional IRA and will be a money saver when you take a distribution from the IRA. After a lifetime of long, hard work, you'll want to be sure about the amount of your retirement nest egg.

You're pretty safe throwing your tax documents away if they're over six years old from the date of filing. Some people like to give them a big send-off in the fireplace, with a toast and hearty "Good riddance!" Shredding is another good option, because these documents contain a lot of confidential information about you. However you go about getting rid of your records, be sure you fully destroy them.

Overall, you can destroy any outdated financial document that has no tax impact. For instance, it's fine to destroy credit card bills over a year old or receipts for items you no longer own. You can also discard paycheck stubs at the end of the year. Just make sure you have verified the totals with a copy of your W-2 so you have a lasting record of earnings.

Records You Can Discard

Here are some documents that you do not need to keep:

- **Canceled checks** (after three years)
- **Household bills** (after one year, except for home improvements)
- **Non-tax related checks** (like graduation money or rebates on consumer items)
- **Pay stubs** (after verifying the totals with your W-2 forms)
- **Quarterly mutual fund statements** (but keep the year-end summary)
- **Records for things you no longer own**
- **Tax documents more than six years old** (except for real estate you still own)

Especially for Small Business Owners

Entrepreneurs are motivated to press on because they "do what they love and love what they do." They are the kind of people who tackle the challenges of creating something new, of finding a whole new way of doing things, of serving customers in a fresher, smarter way. They chase their dream and often catch it.

But operating your own company, no matter what size, isn't all peaches and cream. The tax record-keeping responsibilities of a small business owner are pretty daunting. Calling those responsibilities burdensome is like calling an elephant heavy. A small business owner must take record keeping seriously, because it can make the difference between profitability and potential failure.

THE CHALLENGE

Jane was living a double life. By day, she was an aerospace engineer with a penchant for detail. Every item she kept in her business life had both a place to exist and a good reason for existing. Jane thrived on details. But her home life was a different story. After long hours at the office, it was time to unwind. Jane had piles of clothes and stacks of paper everywhere. She just didn't have the time to sort it all out.

When it came time to file her tax return, Jane panicked. She couldn't find all of her tax records. She thought she had most of them, but after rummaging through stacks of this and piles of that, she couldn't be sure. "What if I missed an expense that I could have deducted or some income that I should have reported?" wondered Jane. She decided that she couldn't afford to live a double life anymore.

THE PLAN

Jane decided that it was time to introduce her business life to her personal life. "I decided that I needed to make the time to find a place for everything—including my tax and financial records," she said.

After clearing out the clutter, Jane went to work on her records. She cleared out a spot in her filing cabinet, bought some folders, and sorted through and found a home for all of her documents. Jane even created special folders for all of her past records to make it easier to remember where they were if she needed them again. "I'm not going to find myself in a messy situation like that again. I file an important document as soon as I receive it," Jane said. "When tax time comes again, I'll be ready."

Don't get us wrong. Just because you have a business doesn't mean you need a record-keeping system that costs a lot of money or that is unwieldy and sophisticated. You can use the same procedures outlined earlier in the chapter to set up a file system (either paper or electronic). But most important of all is to keep your records safe and make sure they are as complete as possible. Remember: Good record keeping can help you document deductions, which add money back to your bottom line.

Small business owners keep many of the same records as individual taxpayers, plus even more records that relate specifically to the business. All receipts, canceled checks, and credit card bills are important records for a small business owner. Anything that relates to operating the business is a candidate for a deduction or credit, so there may be more things to save, such as office expenses, equipment purchases, and long-distance phone records.

Rather than saving everything made of paper, pay special attention to any expenses of $75 or more. Also, make sure you and your employees label things well. Jot on the receipt or in your diary key pieces of information: the amount, date, time, place, and a few words to describe the purpose of the expense. If you lose a receipt or forget to get one, immediately make one of your own and record all the key data. Also, label bank deposit slips. They provide a fast overview of income sources and support your sales records.

Business owners who use a car for business purposes need to maintain an auto diary to record mileage, tolls, and parking fees. You can also save receipts of general upkeep in the diary, or make a journal entry for these items. More is better in the case of auto records.

If your business has an employee payroll, the IRS requires that you file a quarterly payroll tax return. You should keep track of your payroll tax deposits to support the data for each quarterly filing.

It's important to maintain an updated record-keeping system. Procrastination with record keeping can be extremely harmful. Trying to collect and organize a year's worth of business receipts will almost certainly lead to deductions missed and more tax paid than necessary. By conducting a monthly review of your financial and tax records, you can ward off a frustrating year-end accounting experience. Plus, you'll have a better sense of how your business is performing overall.

✓ ─────────────────▶ **Small Business Tax Records Checklist**

Bear this checklist in mind as you create your files:

- ☐ **Asset Purchase Records**—Retain receipts for such items as office and computer equipment, vehicle purchases, machines, furniture, and real estate purchased or leased for business use.
- ☐ **Banking**—We strongly advise that you keep a separate bank account and use a separate credit card and checking account for your business.
- ☐ **Employee Compensation Records**—This applies only if you actually have employees.
- ☐ **Expenses**—At a minimum, make a monthly summary of expenses.
- ☐ **Income Receipt Records**—These records should follow some form of consistent tabulation, such as daily, weekly, or monthly.

You'll find more information on business record keeping in Chapter 8.

Know Your Tax Dates

After all your hard work organizing receipts, invoices, and auto mileage records, the last thing you want to do is miss an important IRS filing deadline. So top off your record-keeping system with one more key reference: the IRS's annual tax calendar. Keep it in a place where it's easy to find, but not annoying. Locations might include inside your record binder, on the side of the filing cabinet, or on the front of the file folder you see most often. Or make it a part of your computer's calendar function.

It's best not to wait until the last day to complete any tax-related transaction. If a due date falls on a Saturday, Sunday, or legal holiday, it moves to the next business day.

IRS Tax Calendar Dates

These are some important dates on the tax calendar.

January 1—Start of tax season.

January 15—For individuals, the fourth payment of the previous tax year's estimated tax is due if you are not paying your income tax for the year through withholding or will not pay in enough tax that way.

January 31—W-2 forms are due from your employer. Provide W-2 forms to your employees, if you have any. Form 1099 is due from payers of interest, dividends, and other specified types of income.

February 15—If you were exempt from income tax withholding for the preceding tax year, you must file a new Form W-4 by today to continue your exemption for the current tax year.

April 15—Tax returns due.

The following, if applicable, are also due

- **Requests for an automatic four-month extension to August 15 to file your tax return.** This does not give you an extension of time to pay any estimated balance due.
- **Preceding tax year IRA contributions, even if you receive an extension.**
- **For individuals, the first payment of your current tax year's estimated tax** (if you are not paying your income tax for the year through withholding or will not pay in enough tax that way).
- **Preceding tax year self-employed retirement plan contributions, unless you filed for an extension.**

June 15—File your preceding year's tax return if you were residing outside of the United States or Puerto Rico on April 15.

For individuals, the second payment of your current tax year's estimated tax is due if you are not paying your income tax for the year through withholding or will not pay in enough tax that way.

August 15—If you filed for an extension, file your return by today and pay any tax, interest, and penalties due.

If necessary, request an additional two-month extension to file your tax return. The request must be postmarked today and is not automatic. You must have a valid reason for needing this extension. If your second extension is approved, your new tax-filing deadline is October 15.

September 15—For individuals, the third payment of your current tax year's estimated tax is due if you are not paying your income tax for the year through withholding or will not pay in enough tax that way.

Don't wait until the last day to complete a tax-related transaction.

October 15—If you filed for and obtained an additional two-month extension in August, file your preceding year's tax return by today and pay any tax, interest, and penalties due.

December 31—Deadline for establishing many self-employed retirement plans.

If you failed to make an election normally required to be made by the date of the return and you filed your return on time, you generally can make the election on an amended return filed by today.

This list provides a snapshot of some important dates on the IRS tax calendar. There may be additional dates that affect your personal tax situation. Be sure you know what dates are important for you. Deadlines have a way of sneaking up and the cost of missing one can be substantial.

the ESSENTIALS

1. Tax planning is a year-round activity. The amount you get out of it depends on the time you put into it.

2. A solid record-keeping system is the foundation for any successful tax-planning strategy.

3. Build a record-keeping system that works for you.

4. Keep tax records for six years.

5. Don't wait for a rainy day to organize. Do it regularly throughout the year.

3 [YOUR RECIPE FOR SUCCESS: The Basic Ingredients of Your Tax Plan]

"Nothing is particularly hard if you divide it into small jobs."
—Henry Ford

Applying Henry Ford's observation to tax planning shows how a task that often seems big and difficult can become smaller and easier. But, as the saying goes, Rome was not built in a day, and you shouldn't think that your tax plan will be either. First, you need to organize yourself, as described in the previous chapter. Then you need to learn more about taxes. Finally, you'll be able to execute a tax plan that works for you.

The second job, learning more about taxes, is a crucial step. A savvy taxpayer knows which life events have tax consequences, and what to do to save the most money. Did you just have a baby? Great! Did you know that you now have another exemption and probably a child tax credit to claim when filing your tax return? Or that you might want to adjust the amount of withholding from your paycheck to take into account the new exemption and child tax credit you'll receive? You can use the money now to pay for diapers, instead of waiting until after you file your tax return for Uncle Sam to return it.

It would be hard for you to take advantage of the tax breaks available in the tax code without first understanding how taxes work. In this chapter we'll describe taxes and taxable income so you can put that knowledge to good use when we tackle adjustments, deductions, credits, and other tax breaks that can change your financial life.

What is Taxable Income?

The term taxable income has several meanings. First, there is "taxable income" as opposed to "**nontaxable income**". Wages you earn from your job are "taxable income" and gifts you receive are "non-taxable income". Unless the law states otherwise, all income is taxable. "Taxable income" also describes the amount that determines your total tax liability before any credits are applied. This is the sum of all taxable income after subtracting adjustments, deductions, and exemptions. Sound confusing? It can be, but stick with us and we'll help you sort it out as we go along.

Examples of Taxable Income

- **Alimony received**
- **Bonuses and stipends**
- **Capital gains** (usually)
- **Commissions, fees, and other earned income**
- **Compensation paid in goods, services, or property**
- **Director fees**
- **Distributions from retirement plans and tax-deferred annuity plans, including Sec. 401(k), Sec. 403(b), and Sec. 457** (some distributions may be nontaxable)
- **Employer contributions to costs of certain fringe benefits**
- **Employer-paid premiums for group-term life insurance over $50,000**
- **Employer supplemental unemployment benefits** (SUB pay)
- **Farm net income**
- **Gains on the sale of business-use property**
- **Gambling and lottery winnings**
- **Income from jury duty**
- **Income from partnerships, estates, and trusts**
- **Income from wage continuation plans, including retirement incentive plans, severance pay, and short-term disability**
- **Interest and dividend income** (most)
- **Net profits from businesses and professions**
- **Net rental income**
- **Prizes**
- **Reimbursements in excess of deductible expenses**
- **Sick pay** (including third-party sick pay)
- **Social Security benefits** (some)
- **State and local tax refunds** (some)

> Unless the law states otherwise, all income is taxable.

- **Stock options** (taxed when nonqualified options are exercised)
- **Strike pay**
- **Unemployment compensation**
- **Union steward fees**
- **Vacation pay**
- **Wages, salaries, tips, and other compensation**

Examples of Income That Is *Not* Taxable

- **Child support payments received**
- **Combat zone pay** (all for enlisted personnel, limited for officers)
- **Damages for personal physical injuries**
- **Disability payments** (if you paid the premiums)
- **Federal income tax refund**
- **Foreign earned income** (but an exclusion may apply)
- **Foster care payments** (qualified)
- **Gain on sale of your principal residence up to $250,000** ($500,000 if filing jointly) **if you meet the requirements**
- **Gifts**
- **Health and accident benefits**
- **Inheritances** (usually)
- **IRA rollovers**
- **Life insurance proceeds** (due to the death of the insured)
- **Municipal bond interest**
- **Roth IRA distributions** (qualified)
- **Scholarships and fellowships** (depending on source and use)
- **Social Security benefits** (some)
- **Veterans' benefits**
- **Welfare benefits**
- **Workers' compensation**

Who Has to File a Tax Return?

Perhaps Benjamin Franklin summed it up best when he said, "In this world nothing can be said to be certain except death and taxes." To fulfill the second part of Franklin's observation, you need to file a tax return. Generally, if you have income, you must file a tax return and pay taxes. There are always exceptions, but we'll focus on those of us who do need to file a tax return. (Even if you die, someone needs to file a tax return for you.)

If you are a U.S. citizen or a resident alien, your gross income filing requirement depends on two things:

- **Your filing status**
- **Your age**

The instructions that come with tax forms, such as Form 1040, contain a chart that can help you determine if your income is high enough to make filing a return a legal necessity.

There is a bright side to filing a tax return: Regardless of how many jobs you've had, how many W-2 forms you received, or how many states you've lived in during the year, you have to file only one federal income tax return.

What's Your Status?

In college, people asked "What's your major?" When you were dating, perhaps you asked "What's your sign?" In tax planning, an important question is, "What's your status?" Or, more accurately, "What is your filing status?" Determining your correct filing status is a critical step in drafting your tax plan-

smart step

You may want to file an income tax return even if you are not otherwise required to file. Filing is the only way you will be able to get a refund of any income tax that may have been withheld or to receive any other refund for which you qualify.

smart step

Use the most favorable filing status for which you qualify.

ning strategy, and it defines what tax breaks you may be eligible for when you file your tax return.

There are five filing statuses. Let's look at each one.

Single—If you're unmarried or legally separated at the end of the tax year and don't meet the requirements for head of household or qualifying widow(er), use this status. Along with this status come higher taxes and a lower standard deduction than either the head of household or qualifying widow(er) statuses.

Married, Filing Jointly—You and your spouse may file a joint return if you and your spouse were still married on the last day of the tax year. Even if only one of you had income, you may file a joint return. This status usually produces a lower tax liability than filing separate returns in part because several deductions and credits are limited or not allowed on separate returns.

Married, Filing Separately—If you and your spouse were married on the last day of the tax year, you may choose to file separate returns. If you choose to file separately, each of you will report only your own income, exemptions, and the deductible expenses you paid. Most married couples file jointly, but there may be situations when filing separately may actually result in tax savings.

Head of Household—Head of household is the most complicated filing status. To qualify, you must be (or be considered as) unmarried on the last day of the tax year and pay more than half the cost of maintaining a household that is the principal home for yourself and at least one qualifying person for over half of the year. If the qualifying person is your parent, the parent need not live with you, but he or she must be your dependent. Tax brackets for this status break about halfway between those for the single status and those for the married filing jointly status. As we mentioned before, this is the most complicated filing status. Carefully examine the qualifications shown in the Form 1040 instructions for this filing status or talk to your tax professional to make sure you are eligible.

Qualifying Widow or Widower with Dependent Child—If your spouse died within the two tax years before the year for which the tax return is being filed, you may be able to use this status. You must be unmarried at the end of the tax year, have a child who qualifies as your dependent, and have borne over half the cost of maintaining your home, which is also the main home of your dependent child. If qualified, you are allowed to use the same tax rate schedule and standard deduction as a married couple filing jointly.

Your Marginal Tax Rate

You know your telephone number and your wedding anniversary, but do you know your marginal tax rate? If you don't know what it is, you won't be able to determine the tax impact of earning an additional dollar of income or finding an extra dollar of deduction. Your **marginal tax rate** is the rate that applies to the top or last dollar of your taxable income. For example, if you are single and have $25,000 of taxable income (meaning, in this case, your total gross income minus any adjustments, your standard deduction or itemized deductions, and your exemption amounts), your marginal tax rate is 15 percent. That means for every extra dollar of taxable income you earn, you will only keep about 85 cents. If you get a nice raise from your boss, and that raise pushes your taxable income above $27,950, your new marginal tax rate is 27 percent. At that rate, if you earn that extra $1 of taxable income, you will only get to keep about 73 cents. As your income grows, your taxes, and the percentage of that income that is consumed by those taxes, also grow due to our graduated income tax rates.

plain talk

The marginal tax rate is the rate that applies to your top or last dollar of income.

America's first income tax was applied in 1861 to help fund the Civil War. Union citizens paid a tax of 3 percent on incomes of $800 or more a year and 5 percent on incomes that exceeded $10,000. Money was tight and incomes were low at the time, so most Northerners earned too little to pay taxes.

Tax brackets have changed dramatically since the days of Abraham Lincoln, but their format hasn't. Our tax system is graduated, meaning that not every dollar of your income is taxed at the same rate. Different portions of your income fall into different brackets, which are assigned higher tax rates as incomes rise. In short, the last dollar you earn will usually be taxed at a higher rate than previous dollars.

Here's a simple 2002 example of how income is taxed. Suppose you're single and your only income is the $40,000 in wages you earned from your job. Let's also assume you have no adjustments (deductions you can take even if you don't itemize) to your income and you use the standard deduction.

▶ How It Works

- **The first $7,700 of your income escapes federal income tax altogether. That's because your standard deduction is $4,700 and your personal exemption amount is $3,000**
- **The next $6,000 of your income is taxed at 10 percent**
- **The next $21,950 is taxed at 15 percent**
- **The final $4,350 is taxed at your highest (marginal) rate of 27 percent**

If someone asks you what bracket you're in, they're usually asking what your marginal tax rate is, which in this case is 27 percent. At this rate, if you receive another $1,000 of income, you'll pay $270 in income tax. Conversely, if you can find a $1,000 deduction, you'll cut your taxes by $270. The following table summarizes this example.

TAXABLE INCOME			
TAXABLE INCOME BRACKETS	**INCOME FROM EXAMPLE**	**TAX RATE**	**TAX**
First $7,700	$ 7,700	0%	$ 0.00
Next $6,000	6,000	10%	600.00
Next $6,001–$27,950	21,950	15%	3,292.50
Next $27,951–$67,700	4,350	27%	1,174.50
Next $67,701–$141,250	0	30%	0.00
Next $141,251–$307,050	0	35%	0.00
Over $307,050	0	38.6%	0.00
Total	**$40,000**		**$5,067.00**

Source: H&R Block

plain talk

Your effective tax rate is the total tax you pay divided by your overall income.

Don't confuse your marginal tax rate with what's called your **effective tax rate**, or the percentage of tax you pay on your overall income. In the example above, your total federal tax is $5,067. Thus your effective tax rate is almost 13 percent ($5,067 divided by $40,000).

For planning purposes, it's your marginal rate that's more useful.

You should also be aware of your combined marginal rate, which is the sum of your federal marginal rate and your state marginal rate. (If your federal marginal rate is 30 percent and your state marginal rate is 6 percent, your combined marginal rate is 36 percent.) Your combined marginal rate determines how much combined tax you'll owe on that extra dollar of income. (If your combined marginal rate is 36 percent, then 36 percent of your additional income will go toward taxes.)

Find your marginal tax rate using the following table.

TAX RATES FOR 2002 TAX RETURNS

TAXABLE INCOME	TAX
SINGLE	
Up to $6,000	10% of every dollar
$6,001–$27,950	$600 plus 15% of amount over $6,000
$27,951–$67,700	$3,892.50 plus 27% of amount over $27,950
$67,701–$141,250	$14,625 plus 30% of amount over $67,700
$141,251–$307,050	$36,690 plus 35% of amount over $141,250
Over $307,050	$94,720 plus 38.6% of amount over $307,050
MARRIED FILING JOINTLY OR QUALIFYING WIDOW(ER)	
Up to $12,000	10% of every dollar
$12,001–$46,700	$1,200 plus 15% of amount over $12,000
$46,701–$112,850	$6,405 plus 27% of amount over $46,700
$112,851–$171,950	$24,265.50 plus 30% of amount over $112,850
$171,951–$307,050	$41,995.50 plus 35% of amount over $171,950
Over $307,050	$89,280.50 plus 38.6% of amount over $307,050
HEAD OF HOUSEHOLD	
Up to $10,000	10% of every dollar
$10,001–$37,450	$1,000 plus 15% of amount over $10,000
$37,451–$96,700	$5,117.50 plus 27% of amount over $37,450
$96,701–$156,600	$21,115 plus 30% of amount over $96,700
$156,601–$307,050	$39,085 plus 35% of amount over $156,600
Over $307,050	$91,742.50 plus 38.6% of amount over $307,050
MARRIED FILING SEPARATELY	
Up to $6,000	10% of every dollar
$6,001–$23,350	$600 plus 15% of amount over $6,000
$23,351–$56,425	$3,202.50 plus 27% of amount over $23,350
$56,426–$85,975	$12,132.75 plus 30% of amount over $56,425
$85,976–$153,525	$20,997.75 plus 35% of amount over $85,975
Over $153,525	$44,640.25 plus 38.6% of amount over $153,525

Source: Internal Revenue Service

Claiming Exemptions

Tax **exemptions** are a great way to reduce your tax bill. You are entitled to claim exemptions, based on certain qualifications, that can result in big tax savings. There are two kinds of exemptions: personal and dependency. Personal exemptions include yourself and your spouse (if you have one). Dependency exemptions include anyone who qualifies as your dependent, usually, but not always, children. An exemption was worth $3,000 for 2002. At that rate, if you were in the 27 percent tax bracket, each exemption you were able to claim would save you $810. If your adjusted gross income exceeds certain amounts, the exemption amount is phased out. For 2003, the exemption amount increases to $3,050.

There are five tests you must meet to claim someone as your dependent. All the tests must be met, but there are two tests in particular—the gross income test and the support test—which may spoil your plans to claim a dependency exemption. A little tax planning before year-end may help you preserve a dependency exemption.

The five dependency tests are:

Gross Income Test—Generally, you may not claim an exemption for your dependent if he or she had gross income equal to or greater than the exemption amount ($3,000 for 2002; $3,050 for 2003). This gross income test does not apply if your child is under age nineteen at the end of the year or is a full-time student under age twenty-four at the end of the year.

When determining whether you can claim an individual other than your child as a dependent (for example, a parent), keep in mind that not all income is included in gross income. Two examples are tax-exempt interest and nontaxable Social Security benefits.

plain talk

An exemption is a standard amount for yourself, your spouse, and each dependent that you may subtract from otherwise taxable income.

Support Test—As a rule, you must provide more than half the dependent's total support to claim a dependency exemption. This test is not difficult to satisfy if you are the primary source of support, such as for a child. But if someone else contributes to the dependent's support or if the dependent contributes to his or her own support, you need to be careful. Before the end of the year, determine how much of the dependent's total support you have provided. If it looks like you are going to fail this test, you may want to consider providing some additional support to push you over the 50 percent mark. Special rules apply to children of divorced or separated parents, and when no one person provides over half the support but two or more persons provide over half the support.

Member of Household or Relationship Test—Persons who are closely related to you (for example, children, grandchildren, parents, grandparents, aunts, uncles, nieces, and nephews related to you by blood) who don't live with you may nonetheless be claimed as your dependents if they pass the other four dependency tests. However, more distant relatives (such as cousins) and persons unrelated to you must be members of your household for the entire year to be claimed as your dependents.

Citizen or Residence Test—Your dependent must be a citizen or national of the United States, or a resident of the United States, Canada, or Mexico during some part of the tax year.

Joint Return Test—Generally, you may not claim an exemption for a dependent who files a joint return. However, if your dependent files a joint return merely to obtain a refund of tax withheld, and neither your dependent nor his or her spouse would have a tax liability if they filed separate returns, you may claim an exemption for that dependent. The dependent must, of course, meet the other four dependency tests.

THE CHALLENGE

Katie, age twenty, is a full-time student studying archaeology at Crosstown University. An enthusiastic student, Katie received a $10,000 nontaxable scholarship in her sophomore year. She also earned and spent $4,000 from an archaeological internship during which she helped discover two dinosaur jawbones. Lisa, Katie's mother, provided $5,000 as Katie's only other support during the year. Lisa wonders if she can still claim an exemption for Katie because she provided only $5,000 out of the total $19,000 Katie used during the year. Can she?

THE PLAN

Lisa isn't sure she can claim Katie as an exemption, so she checks with her tax professional, who explains the tax implications. "Sure," the tax professional assures her, "you certainly can claim Katie as a dependent because you provided more than half of Katie's support." Lisa learned that neither the scholarship nor the expenses it covered are counted in Katie's total support. Although Katie earned more than the $3,000 gross income limit for 2002, the gross income test does not apply because she is a full-time student under age twenty-four.

"That's just what I hoped to hear," Lisa smiles. "I can claim Katie as a dependent for this and hopefully the next few years while she helps solve more prehistoric mysteries."

Pay-As-You-Go Taxes

Under the U.S. income tax system, your income tax is due as you earn the income, not when you file your income tax return. To make this system work more smoothly, employers generally withhold taxes from our paychecks. This method covers the lion's share of taxes collected each year, but other sources of income, such as that from self-employment or investments, may not be subject to automatic withholding. These types of income also require taxes to be paid along the way.

To avoid an underpayment penalty, the IRS generally requires you to timely pay at least the lesser of 90 percent of your current year tax or 100 percent of the total amount of tax shown on your prior year return. Other special rules may apply depending on your prior-year adjusted gross income. You should always keep track of where you stand because your tax situation may change, causing you to either over or underpay. You are able to make adjustments during the year, so smart tax planning may end up saving you some money.

The Art of Withholding

We're sure you'd rather wrestle an alligator than overpay your income taxes. We feel the same way. But each and every year millions of taxpayers overpay their income taxes, often because they've had too much withheld throughout the year. Overpaying your income taxes is like depositing your money into an account that doesn't pay interest and only allows you to make one withdrawal per year. There is no good reason to do this, unless you simply can't keep your hands off of the money and look at it as a forced savings plan.

Take a look at these numbers: In 2002, the IRS processed about 77 million refunds worth a total of about $150 billion. On average, those taxpayers received refunds of about $1,937. Averaged over the year, that's about $37 a week. Think of it as keeping your lunch money instead of giving it to the big kid down the street.

On the other hand, you don't want to make a potentially costly mistake by not having enough income tax withheld or by not paying the right amount of estimated tax. If you don't get it right, you could be facing a penalty in addition to needing to come up with the rest of what you owe.

An important part of your tax plan should be a regular review of your withholding or the amount of your quarterly estimated tax payments. This is a good topic to discuss with your tax professional. With careful planning, you can adjust your withholding or estimated payments to pay just enough to avoid a penalty while paying a balance due, just enough to break even, or enough to provide a refund of the amount you desire.

If you make quarterly estimated income tax payments, you are credited for them only when they are actually rendered to the IRS. If your employer withholds income taxes from your paycheck, those payments are considered to have been made evenly throughout the year, regardless of when they were sent to the IRS. So if your tax situation changes during the year and you think you may be headed for an underpayment penalty, have your employer withhold more during the last few months of the year to make up the difference. If you do this, don't forget to reevaluate your tax situation again after the first of the year to readjust your withholding to the proper amount.

Albert Einstein once said, "The hardest thing in the world to understand is income tax," but you don't need to be a genius to become more tax-savvy.

smart step

Review your tax situation quarterly to determine if you need to adjust your withholding or estimated tax payments to avoid overpaying or underpaying your taxes.

Income taxes may have been hard for Einstein, but they don't have to be that way for you. Detailed, organized records and a working knowledge of tax basics go a long way toward making you what you need and want to be—a taxpayer who takes advantage of all the opportunities in the tax code.

the ESSENTIALS

1   **Savvy tax planning is a year-round activity. The events that occur during the year and the tax-related choices you make will determine your tax bill when you file your return.**

2   **Knowing which income is taxable and which isn't will prevent you from overstating your tax liability.**

3   **Choosing the best filing status that you qualify for can save hundreds of dollars.**

4   **Your marginal tax rate is the rate that applies to your top or last dollar of income.**

5   **Know the five dependency tests so you claim all the dependency exemptions to which you're entitled.**

6   **Adjust your withholding so when you file your return you come close to having no refund and no balance due. If you do, you'll have control of more of your money during the year and avoid underpayment penalties.**

4 [OPPORTUNITY KNOCKS:]

A Roadmap for Form 1040

"Tax avoidance is legal tax planning. Tax evasion is fraud."
—Anonymous

The Form 1040 dates from 1913 and reportedly got its name due to the sequential numbering of forms published by the Bureau of Internal Revenue (as the IRS was known back then). The IRS needed a form to compute the income tax and the Form 1040 was evidently the 1,040th form published. A new edition of Form 1040 has been published every year since, revised to reflect the latest tax law changes.

Now you know when the Form 1040 came into existence and how it was named. The only thing missing is finding out what's actually in it. Why, you ask? Well, it's worthwhile to take a little time to get to know Form 1040 better because it contains many opportunities to reduce your tax bill. But you have to know where to look and what to avoid to make the most of your tax situation.

To help you along the way, we've devised Chapter 4 as a roadmap for Form 1040. By reviewing the form section by section and line by line, you'll have a greater understanding of how to use it to your advantage for tax planning, and the impact those plans will have when your tax return is actually prepared.

A Word on Short Forms

If you're a United States citizen or resident alien, you will file your return on Form 1040EZ or Form 1040A (the so-called short forms) or on the full-blown Form 1040. The IRS instructions that accompany each form have more specific instructions concerning its use.

Here's our suggestion: For purposes of learning about the tax law and how to use it to your advantage, forget the short forms. They have fewer lines than the full Form 1040, in part because they contain fewer opportunities to save money.

OVERVIEW OF U.S. TAX FORMS			
ITEM	**1040EZ**	**1040A**	**1040**
Filing Status	Limited	All	All
Exemptions	Self and spouse only	All	All
Income	Very limited	Limited	All
Adjustments to income	None	Limited	All
Itemized Deductions	No	No	Yes
Standard Deduction	Basic	Full	Full
Other Taxes	None	Limited	All
Tax Credits	EIC for worker with no child only	Limited	All
Payments	Amount withheld on wages or paid with extension only	Limited	All

Source: H&R Block

Form 1040—A Primer

Form 1040 is divided into several distinct sections, each of which is named in the left-hand margin of the form. They are:

- **Filing Status**
- **Exemptions**
- **Income**
- **Adjusted Gross Income**
- **Tax and Credits**
- **Other Taxes**
- **Payments**
- **Refund or Amount You Owe**

Let's take a look at each of these sections and point out some ways to cut your tax liability.

Department of the Treasury—Internal Revenue Service
U.S. Individual Income Tax Return 2002 (99) IRS Use Only—Do not write or staple in this space.

For the year Jan. 1–Dec. 31, 2002, or other tax year beginning , 2002, ending , 20 | OMB No. 1545-0074

Label
(See instructions on page 21.)

Use the IRS label. Otherwise, please print or type.

L A B E L
H E R E

Your first name and initial | Last name | Your social security number

If a joint return, spouse's first name and initial | Last name | Spouse's social security number

Home address (number and street). If you have a P.O. box, see page 21. | Apt. no.

City, town or post office, state, and ZIP code. If you have a foreign address, see page 21.

▲ **Important!** ▲
You **must** enter your SSN(s) above.

Presidential Election Campaign
(See page 21.)

Note. Checking "Yes" will not change your tax or reduce your refund.
Do you, or your spouse if filing a joint return, want $3 to go to this fund? . . . ▶

	You		Spouse
	☐ Yes ☐ No		☐ Yes ☐ No

1

Filing Status

Check only one box.

1 ☐ Single
2 ☐ Married filing jointly (even if only one had income)
3 ☐ Married filing separately. Enter spouse's SSN above and full name here. ▶ _____
4 ☐ Head of household (with qualifying person). (See page 21.) If the qualifying person is a child but not your dependent, enter this child's name here. ▶ _____
5 ☐ Qualifying widow(er) with dependent child (year spouse died ▶). (See page 21.)

2

Exemptions

If more than five dependents, see page 22.

6a ☐ **Yourself.** If your parent (or someone else) can claim you as a dependent on his or her tax return, **do not** check box 6a . . . .
b ☐ **Spouse** . . . .
c Dependents:

(1) First name Last name	(2) Dependent's social security number	(3) Dependent's relationship to you	(4) ✓ if qualifying child for child tax credit (see page 22)
	:		☐
	:		☐
	:		☐
	:		☐
	:		☐

No. of boxes checked on 6a and 6b
No. of children on 6c who:
• lived with you
• did not live with you due to divorce or separation (see page 22)
Dependents on 6c not entered above
Add numbers on lines above ▶ ☐

d Total number of exemptions claimed . . . .

3

Income

Attach Forms W-2 and W-2G here. Also attach Form(s) 1099-R if tax was withheld.

If you did not get a W-2, see page 23.

Enclose, but do not attach, any payment. Also, please use **Form 1040-V.**

7 Wages, salaries, tips, etc. Attach Form(s) W-2 . . . . | 7 |
8a **Taxable** interest. Attach Schedule B if required . . . . | 8a |
b Tax-exempt interest. **Do not** include on line 8a . . . | 8b |
9 Ordinary dividends. Attach Schedule B if required . . . . | 9 |
10 Taxable refunds, credits, or offsets of state and local income taxes (see page 24) . . | 10 |
11 Alimony received . . . . | 11 |
12 Business income or (loss). Attach Schedule C or C-EZ . . . . . . | 12 |
13 Capital gain or (loss). Attach Schedule D if required. If not required, check here ▶ ☐ | 13 |
14 Other gains or (losses). Attach Form 4797 . . . . | 14 |
15a IRA distributions . . | 15a | b Taxable amount (see page 25) | 15b |
16a Pensions and annuities | 16a | b Taxable amount (see page 25) | 16b |
17 Rental real estate, royalties, partnerships, S corporations, trusts, etc. Attach Schedule E | 17 |
18 Farm income or (loss). Attach Schedule F . . . . | 18 |
19 Unemployment compensation . . . . | 19 |
20a Social security benefits . | 20a | b Taxable amount (see page 27) | 20b |
21 Other income. List type and amount (see page 29) _____ | 21 |
22 Add the amounts in the far right column for lines 7 through 21. This is your **total income** ▶ | 22 |

4

Adjusted Gross Income

23 Educator expenses (see page 29) . . . . . | 23 |
24 IRA deduction (see page 29) . . . . . . | 24 |
25 Student loan interest deduction (see page 31) . . | 25 |
26 Tuition and fees deduction (see page 32) . . . | 26 |
27 Archer MSA deduction. Attach Form 8853 . . . | 27 |
28 Moving expenses. Attach Form 3903 . . . . | 28 |
29 One-half of self-employment tax. Attach Schedule SE | 29 |
30 Self-employed health insurance deduction (see page 33) | 30 |
31 Self-employed SEP, SIMPLE, and qualified plans | 31 |
32 Penalty on early withdrawal of savings . . . . | 32 |
33a Alimony paid b Recipient's SSN ▶ | 33a |
34 Add lines 23 through 33a . . . . | 34 |
35 Subtract line 34 from line 22. This is your **adjusted gross income** . . . . ▶ | 35 |

For Disclosure, Privacy Act, and Paperwork Reduction Act Notice, see page 76. Cat. No. 11320B Form **1040** (2002)

1. Filing Status (Lines 1–5)

Choosing the correct and most advantageous filing status is critical to achieving your lowest legal tax liability. Married couples must choose between filing jointly or separately. Unmarried taxpayers, or those who are technically married but are considered unmarried for tax purposes, must choose between the single, head of household, and qualifying widow(er) statuses. Turn back to Chapter 3 for details about each of these filing statuses.

If you're married, a joint return will generally result in a lower tax liability than separate returns, but not always. The safe thing to do is to discuss this choice with your tax professional when you have your return prepared. If your professional thinks it's a close call, ask him or her to complete your return both ways to see which method produces the lower tax liability.

If you're unmarried, or considered unmarried for tax purposes, determine which of the three filing statuses (listed below) you qualify to use. If you qualify for more than one, choose from the list below the most advantageous status for which you qualify. This list is arranged from the most advantageous at the top to the least advantageous at the bottom.

- **Qualifying widow(er)**
- **Head of household**
- **Single**

smart step

If your spouse died during the year, and you didn't remarry before the end of the year, consider filing a joint return with your deceased spouse to take advantage of certain deductions and credits that are not allowed if you file a separate return.

2. Exemptions (Line 6)

Exemptions are worth their weight in gold. For every one that you are eligible to claim, your otherwise taxable income will be reduced by $3,000 for 2002 ($3,050 for 2003). For example, if you are in the 27 percent tax

bracket, each exemption will save you about $810. There are two kinds of exemptions: personal (for you and your spouse, if you have one and are filing jointly) and dependency. Dependency exemptions are usually for family members, but a person doesn't actually have to be related to you to be your dependent. Remember that there are five tests that must be met before you can claim a dependency exemption (see Chapter 3 for more details). And don't forget, if you can be claimed as a dependent on someone else's return, you can't claim a personal exemption on your own return.

3. Income (lines 7–22)

This, in a way, is the good news/bad news section of Form 1040. It's here where you are required to report all income subject to tax. You'll want to make sure you identify all of your taxable income. The information in Chapter 3 can help you determine what's taxable and what's not.

Wages, Salaries, Tips (Line 7)—This is where you report all of your taxable employee compensation.

Interest (Line 8)—Enter taxable interest on line 8a and nontaxable interest on line 8b. Line 8b is for information purposes only; nontaxable interest is not part of your total income on line 22. If you report substantial taxable interest income, you may want to consider investments that generate tax-free income such as municipal bonds or municipal bond funds. Tax-free interest escapes federal income tax and may escape state tax. Consult your tax and financial advisors to determine how tax-free investments could have an impact on your tax and investment planning.

Ordinary Dividends (Line 9)—Ordinary dividends are the portion of the profits earned by an organization that are paid out to shareholders.

Taxable Refunds, Credits, or Offsets (Line 10)—If you overpaid your state or local income tax on a previous year's return, you need to determine if some, all, or none of your refund is taxable. Generally, refunds are tax-free for most taxpayers. If you didn't itemize your deductions on the prior year federal return, your refund isn't taxable. If you did itemize, part or all of the refund still may not be taxable.

Alimony Received (Line 11)—Alimony you receive is generally taxable income to you if it is deductible by the payer. To qualify as alimony, the payments must meet certain requirements. However, other payments you may receive from a former spouse are not considered to be alimony and are therefore not taxable income. Examples include child support payments and payments made that are not required by the decree or agreement. If your former spouse is required to pay both alimony and child support and pays less than the total amount required, the payments are allocated first to child support and then to alimony. Only the portion allocated to alimony is taxable income.

Business Income or Loss (Line 12)—A net loss from your own trade or business can be subtracted from your other income if you meet certain requirements. If the loss exceeds your other income, you may be able to use the loss to reduce taxable income in previous or future years. Compute income or loss from your business on Schedule C, or Schedule C-EZ if you qualify to use this simpler form.

Capital Gain or Loss (Line 13)—You can deduct up to $3,000 of net capital losses per year. Any losses not deductible because of this limitation may be carried over to future years. Generally, you must complete Schedule D to compute your net capital gain or loss. However, if your only capital gains for the year are capital gain distributions from mutual funds and you have no capital losses, the gains can be reported directly on Form 1040 without filing Schedule D (which is complex). Long-term capital gains are usually taxed at a lower rate than other income.

smart step

If you have no earned income but receive taxable alimony, you may contribute to an IRA. Alimony received is considered earned income for IRA purposes. See Chapter 7 for more information about IRAs.

smart step

Prior to selling any capital assets, make sure you understand the tax consequences. The amount of tax on capital gains can vary depending on how long you owned the asset you sold, what that asset was, and your tax bracket.

Other Gains or Losses (Line 14)—Did you sell or exchange any assets used in a trade or business or as rental property? If so, you will report the gain or loss here. You'll need to complete Form 4797, which is sort of like a Schedule D with an attitude. Your best bet is to get professional assistance.

IRA Distributions (Line 15)—The rules for determining how much of an IRA distribution is taxable are complex. People often report more or less taxable income than required. Underreporting could result in payment of unneccesary penalties and interest. The advice of a tax professional is well worth your while, at least for the first year you take money from an IRA.

Pensions and Annuities (Line 16)—If you receive distributions from pensions or annuities, report them here. Generally, pensions are fully taxable when you have recovered all of your own after-tax contributions or if you made no after-tax contributions to the retirement fund. Annuity payments usually consist of both a return of your investment and earnings on your investment, and they are normally partly taxable.

Rental Real Estate, Royalties, Partnerships, etc. (Line 17)—On this line, enter your income or loss from real estate rentals, royalties, partnerships, S corporations, and trusts. You'll need to complete Schedule E for this type of income or loss. If you have rental real estate, keep good records of your income and expenses.

Farm Income (Line 18)—If you are a farmer, report any farm-related income or loss here. All income from farming is included, and all ordinary and necessary farming expenses are deductible. You'll need to complete Schedule F before making an entry on line 18. Farmers are subject to self-employment tax, but they receive a deduction for one-half of this tax on line 29.

Unemployment Compensation (Line 19)—Unemployment compensation received under a state or federal program is fully taxable. To avoid having a balance due when your tax return is completed, you can probably elect to have income tax withheld from your unemployment compensation payments.

Social Security Benefits (Line 20)—Anywhere from 0 to 85 percent of your benefits is taxable. A worksheet that comes with the IRS instructions for line 20 or your tax professional can help you compute the taxable portion of your benefits.

Other Income (Line 21)—As we described in Chapter 3, all income is taxable unless the law specifically states otherwise. Taxable income that doesn't fit anywhere else on Form 1040, or any other form or schedule that you might be required to attach to it, is reported on line 21. Examples include jury duty fees, hobby income, certain damage awards, and gambling winnings.

Total Income (Line 22)—This line lets you see your total income potentially subject to income tax. Now, we can start to look for ways to shelter some of that income from the IRS.

There are two types of IRAs: traditional and Roth. While both are excellent retirement-savings vehicles, their different tax treatments will make one better than the other for you, depending on a variety of factors.

4. Adjustments (Lines 23–35)

Adjustments are deductions you can take whether or not you itemize, and there's quite a list of them. Take every one for which you qualify.

Educator Expenses (Line 23)—If you're a teacher, counselor, administrator, or school aide and you spent some of your own money to purchase classroom supplies, you can probably deduct up to $250 of your out-of-pocket expenses.

IRA Deduction (Line 24)—Contributions to a traditional IRA may be fully or partly deductible. If you qualify, you may deduct contributions to a traditional IRA made up to and including April 15 on your previous year's return. For 2002, the maximum contribution and deduction rose to $3,000 ($3,500 if you are age fifty or older) and will continue to increase annually for the next few years. Be sure to read Chapter 7 for more information about IRAs.

Student Loan Interest Deduction (Line 25)—You can deduct up to $2,500 of interest you paid on student loans. The deduction can be taken for interest paid on almost any type of loan that is taken to pay for qualified higher education expenses (including tuition, room and board, fees, and books) for yourself, your spouse, or someone who was your dependent when the loan was taken out. You cannot deduct interest on any loans that you are deducting elsewhere on your tax return, loans you receive from a relative, loans that were not used exclusively for qualified education expenses, or loans from company retirement plans. Income limitations apply. For more information see the worksheet for this line in the Form 1040 instructions.

Tuition and Fees Deduction (Line 26)—For 2002, you may deduct up to $3,000 of qualified higher education tuition and fees you paid for yourself, your spouse, or your dependents. But before you do that, check with your tax professional. It's quite possible that other tax breaks, such as the Hope credit or the lifetime learning credit, may serve you better. See Chapter 9 for more information about education-related tax breaks.

Archer MSA Deduction (Line 27)—A medical savings account (MSA) is available to certain employees and self-employed individuals who maintain high-deductible health care plans. Contributions to an MSA are deductible and withdrawals are tax-free when used to pay qualified medical expenses. Compute your MSA deduction on Form 8853. Your financial advisor can help you determine if you qualify for an MSA and if it is a wise option for you to consider.

Moving Expenses (Line 28)—If you moved for work-related reasons, you may be able to deduct your moving expenses. Your new principal place of work must be at least fifty miles farther from your old home than your old home was from your former place of work. The moving expense deduction is computed on Form 3903, which will also tell you which expenses are deductible, which are not, and how long you must work at your new job or self-employment.

One-Half of Self-Employment Tax (Line 29)—If you are self-employed, this tax is the equivalent of Social Security and Medicare taxes paid by employees and employers. For 2002, the self-employment tax is 15.3 percent of the first $84,900 of self-employment income and 2.9 percent of income over $84,900. You may deduct one-half of the self-employment tax that is entered on line 56 of Form 1040. If you are in the 27 percent bracket, the 50 percent deduction saves you $135 for each $1,000 in self-employment tax you pay. The Social Security wage base increases to $87,000 for 2003.

Self-Employed Health Insurance Deduction (Line 30)—For 2002, qualified self-employed taxpayers can deduct 70 percent of the cost of health insurance for themselves and their families. Any amount not deductible here is added to other medical expenses on Schedule A. This adjustment will get even better for 2003 and beyond as self-employed taxpayers will be allowed to deduct 100 percent of what they pay for qualified medical insurance.

Self-Employed, SEP, SIMPLE, and Qualified Plans (Line 31)—As a self-employed individual, you may establish a qualified retirement plan for yourself and your employees. These are often known as Keogh plans. You can also establish a less complicated retirement plan known as a simplified employee pension (SEP). Generally, for 2002, you can contribute up to $40,000 to a Keogh plan or SEP, or up to $7,000 to a SIMPLE plan. SIMPLE plans generally must be established by October 1, and Keogh plans must be opened by

smart step

If you are receiving unemployment compensation or if any of your Social Security benefits are taxable, consider electing to have income tax withheld to avoid having a balance due when you file your tax return.

THE CHALLENGE

Rachel, a recent college graduate, always relied on her parents to prepare her tax return. Having recently moved across the country to start her first real job as a kindergarten teacher, Rachel realized that she was on her own for many things, including taxes. "I did some research and came to a conclusion—that I needed some help," Rachel explained. "There were a lot of forms that I needed to complete and many options to consider. For example, a friend told me that I might be able to claim a deduction for my moving expenses. I hadn't even thought about things like that."

THE PLAN

Rachel did some more research and found a local tax professional that had a great reputation in the community for taking care of her clients. "During our appointment, my tax professional explained to me that although I did not have enough deductions to itemize this year, I did qualify for several adjustments. Adjustments are similar to deductions, but you don't need to itemize to claim them." Rachel's tax professional pointed out that she could deduct the interest she was paying on a student loan she had used to pay for her college tuition, and that she could also deduct up to $250 that she had spent on supplies to get her classroom prepared for her students. "I guess you never stop learning," Rachel said. "I learned that it pays to find someone that you can trust—especially with your financial matters."

December 31 in order to deduct contributions for the current year. An SEP must be opened on or before April 15 of the following year (or by the extended due date of your return if you applied for an extension). Your contributions to these plans can be made as late as April 15 (or the extended due date of your return if later) in order to qualify as an adjustment for the previous tax year.

Penalty on Early Withdrawal of Savings (Line 32)—Did you have to make an early withdrawal from a time deposit during the year? If so, you may have had to forfeit some interest and/or pay a penalty. You will report the full amount of the interest on line 8, and deduct the amount of interest you had to forfeit on line 32. The amount of the deduction will be shown in Box 2 of your Form 1099-INT, which will be given to you by your bank or financial institution.

Alimony Paid (Line 33)—Payments for alimony or separate maintenance that you made either under a court decree of divorce or separation, or under a decree of support, are fully deductible here if they meet the requirements. You will need to provide the recipient's Social Security number to claim this deduction. Child support payments are not deductible.

Add Lines 23 through 33a (Line 34)—If no specific line is provided for an adjustment, describe the item and put the amount here. Sound strange? Well, it may be, but there are some adjustments that are available and there's no good place to put them. These adjustments include items such as jury duty fees that you had to report as income earlier in the form. If you had to turn over the fees to your employer in order to receive your regular pay, they are deductible here. A list of these "write-in" adjustments can be found in the Form 1040 instructions for line 34.

smart step

If you stopped taking the student loan interest deduction because your payments ran for more than sixty months, you can start taking it again on your 2002 return because the sixty-month rule has been repealed.

Tax and Credits	**36**	Amount from line 35 (adjusted gross income)	**36**
	37a	Check if: ☐ **You** were 65 or older, ☐ Blind; ☐ **Spouse** was 65 or older, ☐ Blind. Add the number of boxes checked above and enter the total here . . . . ▶ **37a**	

Standard Deduction for-

- People who checked any box on line 37a or 37b **or** who can be claimed as a dependent, see page 34.
- All others:

Single, $4,700

Head of household, $6,900

Married filing jointly or Qualifying widow(er), $7,850

Married filing separately, $3,925

b	If you are married filing separately and your spouse itemizes deductions, or you were a dual-status alien, see page 34 and check here . . . . . . ▶ **37b** ☐	
38	**Itemized deductions** (from Schedule A) **or** your **standard deduction** (see left margin) .	**38**
39	Subtract line 38 from line 36	**39**
40	If line 36 is $103,000 or less, multiply $3,000 by the total number of exemptions claimed on line 6d. If line 36 is over $103,000, see the worksheet on page 35	**40**
41	**Taxable income.** Subtract line 40 from line 39. If line 40 is more than line 39, enter -0-	**41**
42	**Tax** (see page 36). Check if any tax is from: **a** ☐ Form(s) 8814 **b** ☐ Form 4972 . .	**42**
43	**Alternative minimum tax** (see page 37). Attach Form 6251	**43**
44	Add lines 42 and 43 . . . . ▶	**44**
45	Foreign tax credit. Attach Form 1116 if required	**45**
46	Credit for child and dependent care expenses. Attach Form 2441	**46**
47	Credit for the elderly or the disabled. Attach Schedule R .	**47**
48	Education credits. Attach Form 8863	**48**
49	Retirement savings contributions credit. Attach Form 8880 .	**49**
50	Child tax credit (see page 39)	**50**
51	Adoption credit. Attach Form 8839	**51**
52	Credits from: **a** ☐ Form 8396 **b** ☐ Form 8859 . .	**52**
53	Other credits. Check applicable box(es): **a** ☐ Form 3800 **b** ☐ Form 8801 **c** ☐ Specify _____	**53**
54	Add lines 45 through 53. These are your **total credits**	**54**
55	Subtract line 54 from line 44. If line 54 is more than line 44, enter -0- . . . . . ▶	**55**

Other Taxes	**56**	Self-employment tax. Attach Schedule SE	**56**
	57	Social security and Medicare tax on tip income not reported to employer. Attach Form 4137 . .	**57**
	58	Tax on qualified plans, including IRAs, and other tax-favored accounts. Attach Form 5329 if required	**58**
	59	Advance earned income credit payments from Form(s) W-2	**59**
	60	Household employment taxes. Attach Schedule H	**60**
	61	Add lines 55 through 60. This is your **total tax** . . . . ▶	**61**

Payments	**62**	Federal income tax withheld from Forms W-2 and 1099 . .	**62**
If you have a qualifying child, attach Schedule EIC.	**63**	2002 estimated tax payments and amount applied from 2001 return .	**63**
	64	**Earned income credit (EIC)**	**64**
	65	Excess social security and tier 1 RRTA tax withheld (see page 56)	**65**
	66	Additional child tax credit. Attach Form 8812 . . .	**66**
	67	Amount paid with request for extension to file (see page 56)	**67**
	68	Other payments from: **a** ☐ Form 2439 **b** ☐ Form 4136 **c** ☐ Form 8885	**68**
	69	Add lines 62 through 68. These are your **total payments** . . . . . . ▶	**69**

Refund	**70**	If line 69 is more than line 61, subtract line 61 from line 69. This is the amount you **overpaid**	**70**
Direct deposit? See page 56 and fill in 71b, 71c, and 71d.	**71a**	Amount of line 70 you want **refunded to you** . . . . . . ▶	**71a**
▶ **b**	Routing number	▶ **c** Type: ☐ Checking ☐ Savings	
▶ **d**	Account number		
	72	Amount of line 70 you want **applied to your 2003 estimated tax** ▶	**72**

Amount You Owe	**73**	**Amount you owe.** Subtract line 69 from line 61. For details on how to pay, see page 57 ▶	**73**
	74	Estimated tax penalty (see page 57)	**74**

Third Party Designee

Do you want to allow another person to discuss this return with the IRS (see page 58)? ☐ **Yes.** Complete the following. ☐ **No**

Designee's name ▶	Phone no. ▶ ( )	Personal identification number (PIN) ▶

Sign Here

Under penalties of perjury, I declare that I have examined this return and accompanying schedules and statements, and to the best of my knowledge and belief, they are true, correct, and complete. Declaration of preparer (other than taxpayer) is based on all information of which preparer has any knowledge.

Joint return? See page 21.

Keep a copy for your records.

Your signature	Date	Your occupation	Daytime phone number ( )
Spouse's signature. If a joint return, **both** must sign.	Date	Spouse's occupation	

Paid Preparer's Use Only

Preparer's signature ▶	Date	Check if self-employed ☐	Preparer's SSN or PTIN
Firm's name (or yours if self-employed), address, and ZIP code ▶		EIN	
		Phone no. ( )	

60

5. Tax and Credits (Lines 36–55)

I n this portion of Form 1040, you further reduce your income subject to tax by your standard deduction or itemized deductions and by your exemption amount. Then you compute your tax using one of several available methods. You may also be able to reduce your tax dollar-for-dollar by the use of some great money savers called tax credits. All the credits reported on this portion of Form 1040 are nonrefundable, meaning that if the credit exceeds your tax, the excess is not refunded to you. Refundable credits are reported in the Payments section, so stay tuned.

Standard Deduction or Itemized Deductions (Line 38)—There is nothing wrong with claiming the standard deduction. Electing to take this deduction doesn't mean that you were too lazy to take the time to itemize your deductions. It is designed to be used when your itemized deductions for the year are less than the standard deduction for your filing status. When this happens, you actually get credit for more than you spent on deductible expenses during the year. Sounds pretty smart, doesn't it? If you do itemize or think you might benefit from doing so, make sure you look at the next chapter for more useful information.

Alternative Minimum Tax (Line 43)—Congress enacted the alternative minimum tax (AMT) "to ensure that no taxpayer with substantial economic income can avoid significant tax liability by using exclusions, deductions, and credits." The reality is that more taxpayers are subject to the AMT, including some who do not have high levels of income and some who are not using a lot of tax breaks. To find out more about the AMT, see Form 6251 and its instructions.

Foreign Tax Credit (Line 45)—This credit is used to alleviate double taxation for those who must pay foreign tax and United States income tax on the same income. For example, if you have investments in foreign securities on which you must pay foreign and U.S. income tax, you can treat the tax paid as an itemized

**fast
fact**

A tax credit is almost always worth more than an item- ized deduction because the credit offsets your tax liabil- ity dollar-for- dollar.

deduction or claim this credit. You'll probably want to claim the credit, because it reduces your tax liability dollar-for-dollar. Complete Form 1116 if necessary. Generally, if your credit is $300 or less ($600 or less on a joint return), you can just enter your credit directly on line 45.

Child and Dependent Care Credit (Line 46)—If you pay for child or dependent care while you work, you may be able to claim a tax credit on your return. To qualify for this credit, you (and your spouse, if you're married) must generally be working at the time you incurred the expenses. The care must be for your child (under thirteen when the care was provided), for a disabled spouse, or for a dis- abled dependent. Complete Form 2441 to compute your allowable credit.

Credit for the Elderly or Disabled (Line 47)—You may be eligible for this tax credit if you are age sixty-five or older or you are disabled. In either case, your income must be quite low to qualify. See Schedule R for more information.

Education Credits (Line 48)—Obtaining a higher education is more affordable thanks to the Hope credit and the lifetime learning credit, which help defray higher education costs. The Hope credit can be worth up to $1,500 for each qualified student in the first two years of college. The lifetime learning credit can be worth up to $1,000 a year and is not limited to the first two years of col- lege, but the $1,000 limit applies to the family, not to each student. See Chap- ter 9 for more information about these valuable credits and several other tax-related education benefits.

Retirement Savings Contribution Credit (Line 49)—New for 2002 is the saver's tax credit. If your modified adjusted gross income is $50,000 or less (married filing jointly), $37,500 or less (head of household), or $25,000 or less (all other filing statuses), you may claim a credit for up to 50 percent of your contributions to qualified retirement plans. Your credit percentage depends on your adjusted gross income. Compute your credit on Form 8880.

Child Tax Credit (Line 50)—The IRS allows a $600 credit for each dependent child under seventeen. If your adjusted gross income exceeds $75,000 on single or head of household return, or $110,000 on a joint return, this credit is phased out.

Adoption Credit (Line 51)—The adoption credit was created to assist with the high costs associated with adoption. The credit can be worth up to $10,000 per adoption. Qualified expenses include adoption fees, court costs, attorneys' fees, travel expenses, and other expenses directly related to the adoption. An eligible child for purposes of the credit must be under age eighteen, or physically or mentally incapable of self-care. The credit is phased out gradually if your modified adjusted gross income exceeds $150,000. Compute your credit on Form 8839.

6. Other Taxes (Lines 56–61)

ncome tax isn't the only tax computed on Form 1040. This section of the form (another bad news section) is for entering a variety of other taxes you may owe.

Self-Employment Tax (Line 56)—If your self-employment income is $400 or more, you may be liable for self-employment tax. The self-employment tax rate of 15.3 percent includes 12.4 percent Social Security tax and 2.9 percent Medicare tax. For 2002, the Social Security tax applies to the first $84,900 of self-employment income (minus any wages you have subject to Social Security tax). Only the Medicare part of the tax applies to self-employment income over $84,900. Half of your self-employment tax is deductible on line 29. Compute your self-employment tax on Schedule SE.

Social Security and Medicare Tax on Tip Income Not Reported to Employer (Line 57)—If you didn't report to your employer all your cash tips

smart step

If your employer offers child-care assistance as part of your benefits package, check out that option carefully. The tax-savings may be greater than those offered by the child-care credit.

that the law requires, you generally must pay Social Security and Medicare tax on the unreported tips here. Use Form 4137.

Tax on Qualified Plans, and Other Tax-Favored Accounts (line 58)—You may have to pay a variety of penalty taxes if you don't follow all of the rules concerning tax-sheltered retirement plans, Archer MSAs, and Coverdell ESAs. The penalties are designed to encourage compliance with the rules governing the plans, and there may be exceptions to the penalties. The penalties generally are computed on Form 5329. The form's instructions explain in detail the various exceptions to the penalties. You'll also want to read Chapter 7 for more information about these plans.

Advance Earned Income Credit Payments (Line 59)—If you received advance earned income payments during the year, your Form W-2 will show the amount you received in box 9. Enter this amount on line 59.

Household Employment Taxes (Line 60)—If you paid wages to household employees, you may be liable for FICA (Social Security, Medicare) and FUTA (unemployment taxes). Compute these taxes on Schedule H if you're subject to them.

7. Payments (Lines 62–69)

This section of the Form 1040 records all your tax payments and any **refundable credits** for which you're eligible.

Federal Income Tax Withheld (Line 62)—Double-check your Forms W-2 and 1099 to make sure you report all the tax withheld from your income.

Estimated Tax Payments (Line 63)—Enter here all estimated payments you made during the year. Also check last year's return to see if you designated all or part of your refund to pay this year's tax. If so, include that amount here as well.

Earned Income Credit (Line 64)—If your earned income and adjusted gross income are less than $34,178 (two or more children), $30,201 (one child), or $12,060 (no children), you may be able to take the earned income credit. These amounts are for joint filers. They are $1,000 less for other filing statuses. Note that you cannot take the credit if you use the married filing separately status.

Excess Social Security and Tier 1 RRTA Tax Withheld (Line 65)—If you worked for more than one employer and your combined pay exceeded $84,900 for 2002, too much Social Security tax or Tier 1 RRTA tax may have been withheld from your paychecks. Enter the excess on line 65. The Social Security wage base increases to $87,000 for 2003.

Additional Child Tax Credit (Line 66)—If you were entitled to a child tax credit and your credit was limited by the amount of your tax liability, you may qualify for the refundable additional child tax credit. Check out Form 8812 and its instructions to see if you qualify.

8. Refund or Amount You Owe (Lines 70–74)

At last, the bottom line. If you owe a great deal and can't pay right away, see Chapter 10 for how to arrange a payment plan with the IRS and for other ideas about getting the debt paid.

Direct Deposit of Refund (Line 71)—Let's face it: Nobody wants to wait for a refund, especially in this "real-time" age of immediate gratification. So if you have a refund coming, have the IRS send your money directly to your checking or savings account. Direct deposit can save you time and should help you get

smart step

Obtain a Social Security number for your children soon after they are born. You'll need a Social Security number to claim a dependency exemption, head of household filing status, and certain credits when filing your return.

smart step

Consider using your refund to increase your retirement savings or to fund an education savings plan for your child.

your money at least several days sooner than if you had to wait for a check to arrive in the mail.

You're Getting a Refund. Now What?

A large refund is a bit like found money: If it's unbudgeted, you can use it any way you like. But before you make a down payment on a motorcycle or book a world cruise, consider how the money might be put to good use in your long-range financial plan. Perhaps you could pay down some high-interest credit card debt. Maybe you can contribute to an IRA or invest in an education savings plan for your child.

A large refund also means that you have been giving the government an interest-free loan for the past year. Think about changing your withholding and/or your estimated payments to reduce the refund next year. For more information on withholding and estimated payments, see Chapter 3.

Estimated Tax Penalty (Line 74)—You may owe an underpayment penalty if your tax liability exceeds the amount you have paid through withholding and estimated tax payments by $1,000 or more. Generally, you won't owe a penalty if you've paid the lesser of 90 percent of this year's tax or 100 percent of last year's tax.

Hopefully this trip through Form 1040 has shown you at least a few money-saving opportunities. Keep reading for more information on many of the topics touched on here.

the ESSENTIALS

1 Form 1040 is the document most of us use for filing our income tax returns.

2 The long form (Form 1040) contains more tax-saving opportunities than the short forms.

3 Choosing the correct and most advantagous filing status is a key to paying the lowest legal tax liability.

4 Be certain that you report all taxable income and claim every exemption, deduction, and credit to which you are entitled.

5 If you have a large refund, consider using the windfall to enhance your financial situation by making an IRA contribution or other investment. Also consider reducing your withholding or estimated payments.

5 [ADDITION BY SUBTRACTION: Using Deductions and Tax Credits to Your Advantage]

"I'm proud to be paying taxes in the U.S. The only thing is, I could be just as proud for half the money."

—Arthur Godfrey

fast fact

An amount owed to you that you are unable to collect may be deductible even if you don't itemize. See IRS Publications 535 and 550 for more information.

Most of us have probably heard of so called "fuzzy" or "whole" math. In this type of math, credit could be given for guessing at an answer or trying to understand a concept without ever actually determining the right answer. The use of this type of math may be a hotbed for debate among educators, but it is safe to say there is no room for guesswork in developing and implementing your tax plan. "Close enough" does not count in the subject of taxes; the right answer is a must. Luckily, the math required is just the basics: addition, subtraction, and a little bit of multiplication.

Deductions, exemptions, and credits can reduce your tax liability. We've devoted this chapter to describing many of the tax breaks available to you. We'll help you add it all up so you can subtract as much as possible from your tax liability.

Let's get started.

Using Subtraction to Add to Your Wealth

Once you've determined your total income potentially subject to tax, the next step is to maximize your use of the various tax breaks to reduce your tax liability to its legal minimum. This process takes place in four steps. Here they are in the order they appear on good old Form 1040.

- **Adjustments to Income**—These are deductions (a deduction, loosely defined, is a reduction of income that would otherwise be subject to tax) that you may take *in addition* to the standard deduction or your itemized deductions. You may have heard of "above the line" deductions. That is what we are talking about here. Adjustments to income include alimony you paid, certain IRA contributions, student loan interest, moving expenses, and much more. We mentioned these in Chapter 4 during our stroll through Form 1040. Once you have subtracted your adjustments from your income, you have your **adjusted gross income** (AGI), a tax term you may have heard, but may have had a hard time defining. Understanding adjusted gross income is important because it determines, for example, whether you can deduct traditional IRA contributions, whether your exemptions and/or itemized deductions are reduced, and whether you may claim certain credits, such as the child tax credit, earned income credit, and others.

- **Standard Deduction or Itemized Deductions**—You must choose between the two, and of course you'll generally choose the one that saves you the most money. Both the standard deduction and itemized deductions are discussed in this chapter.

- **Exemption Amounts**—These are standard amounts you may subtract from otherwise taxable income. The exemption amount for 2002 is generally $3,000 ($3,050 for 2003) each for yourself, your spouse, and each of your dependents. However, if your 2002 AGI exceeds $103,000, ($104,625 for 2003) your exemption amount may be reduced. We discussed personal and dependency exemptions in Chapters 3 and 4.

- **Credits**—Once you have subtracted your adjustments, standard deduction or itemized deductions, and exemption amounts from your otherwise taxable income, you can compute your tax. But we're not done lowering your tax liability just yet. You can still claim some credits, which are valuable tax savers because they reduce your tax dollar-for-dollar—a $100 credit reduces your tax by $100. Some of the more common credits are the education credits, the child tax credit, the child-care credit, the adoption credit, the foreign tax credit, and, new for 2002, a credit for contributions you make to certain retirement plans. We provide details about all these credits and several more in this chapter.

plain talk

Adjusted gross income (AGI) is your gross income reduced by any adjustments. Adjustments are expenses that may be deducted from your gross income even if you don't itemize deductions.

Take a look at your itemized deductions every year even if you generally take the standard deduction. If you don't evaluate which option is better for you, you may be paying more tax than necessary.

Deciphering Deductions

A key to your tax-planning strategy is to understand both the standard deduction and itemized deductions, and how to know which is better for you. What's more, when you learn what you can and can't deduct, you'll also learn what records you need to keep.

When you file your federal income tax return on Form 1040, you either take the standard deduction or itemize your deductions. Itemizing your deductions is generally beneficial only if your qualified expenses total more than the standard deduction for your filing status.

The standard deduction changes each year to adjust for inflation. As the standard deduction continues to increase, many taxpayers may not realize additional benefits from itemizing their deductions.

But if you do have enough qualified expenses to allow you to itemize, and many taxpayers do but don't realize it, it's smart to keep track of those expenses and to use Schedule A, Itemized Deductions. The reduction in your tax bill can be significant.

What Can You Deduct?

The IRS wants you to take all the deductions to which you are entitled, and even points you in the right direction. But it is your responsibility to claim those deductions on your tax return. With some research, you'll leave no itemized deduction undeducted.

Let's take a look at a list of common itemized deductions. You'll record these deductions on Schedule A, Itemized Deductions.

Medical Expenses—The costs of medical and dental care continue to rise, but you may be able to ease some of the pain by deducting them. You can deduct only the amount of unreimbursed expenses that totals more than 7.5 percent of your AGI. Toward the end of the year, take a look at the total amount of your medical expenses. If it doesn't look like the total will exceed 7.5 percent of your AGI, see if you can delay paying any more medical expenses until after the first of the new year. If you find that you're already over the 7.5 percent minimum or on the verge of exceeding the threshold, pay more of your medical bills before year-end to increase your deduction.

Most medical and dental expenses are deductible, including the cost of pre-scription medicines, mental health expenses, stop-smoking and doctor-prescribed weight-loss programs, drug and alcohol treatment programs, and, of course, doctor visits and hospital expenses. Some medical expenses that are not deductible include the cost of over-the-counter medicines, most cosmetic pro-cedures, and illegal operations and treatments.

Taxes—Unfortunately, most of the taxes we pay aren't deductible. Here's the list of taxes that *are* deductible:

- **Foreign income taxes** (but taking the foreign tax credit is almost always a smarter tax move—see Foreign Tax Credit later in this chapter)
- **Personal property taxes to the extent that the tax is based on the value of the property** (To be deductible, such taxes must be charged on an annual basis, even if collected more or less often)
- **State and local income taxes**
- **State, local, and foreign real estate taxes**

Interest You Paid—Qualified residence interest, investment interest, and busi-ness interest are deductible. Unfortunately, **personal interest** (inter-est on personal debt that isn't qualified residence interest, interest on business

plain talk

Nondeductible personal inter-est is interest that is not qual-ified residence interest or in-terest incurred on investments, student loans, business loans, or passive activities.

loans, or investment interest) is not deductible. But certain student loan interest is deductible even if you don't itemize.

- **Qualified residence interest** is one deductible expense people talk about when they say how it really pays to own a home. Often, this is the deduction that will enable people to itemize their deductions. In addition to interest included in your monthly payments, you can deduct points on a mortgage for your main home, a mortgage prepayment penalty, and interest on an equity line of credit secured by your home. Be aware that limits to your deduction may apply. Since your home may also be your biggest investment, we'll go into even more detail about this subject in Chapter 6.

- **Qualified investment interest** is the interest expense you paid on investment-related loans. This interest is deductible only to the extent of your investment income. We'll look closer at this deduction in Chapter 6.

Gifts to Charity—If you itemize deductions, you can deduct financial gifts to qualified charitable and religious organizations. The federal government will, in effect, make part of the donation for you. If your marginal tax rate is 30 percent and you donate $100 to a qualified charity, the gift only costs you $70, because the $100 charitable deduction reduces your tax liability by $30.

As with many other financial moves, timing is important. If you're considering making a gift to your favorite charity, make it before the end of the year to add to your itemized deductions. If you normally give a monthly tithe or offering to your place of worship, make your January contribution at the end of December to increase your deduction by the same amount.

Donations of money and property to qualified organizations are deductible. However, not everything you do for charity or your religious organizations is deductible. For example, you can't deduct the value of your time, no matter how much you would charge a paying customer for the same service. You also can't deduct the value of donating the *use* of property. For example, if you donate your week in a time-share resort to a church auction, you generate no deduction regardless of the value of the week on the open market.

Giving Stock

If you own property (such as stock) that has appreciated, and you have owned it for more than a year, there may be a good reason to give it away instead of cash. You can deduct the current value of the stock rather than what you originally paid for it. You'll also avoid paying tax on the gain that built up during the time you owned it. If, on the other hand, your stock had declined in value, you could sell the stock and deduct your loss. Then, you can give the money to charity and take a deduction for the donation too.

Casualty and Theft Losses—Was your car vandalized or stolen? If so, you may be entitled to a deduction. Deductible casualty losses include physical damage to your property caused by sudden, unexpected, or unusual events such as fire, wind, bursting water pipes, tornadoes, and even volcanic eruption. Deductible theft losses involve crimes such as robbery, larceny, embezzlement, and even blackmail, and must be in violation of local laws in the place where the act occurred. Once the amount of your loss has been established, it must be reduced by reimbursements you received or may receive in the future, such as insurance or other compensation. The loss must also be more than $100 and is further reduced by 10 percent of your AGI. If you incurred a casualty or theft loss, Form 4684 and its instructions will guide you through the rules regarding this deduction.

Miscellaneous Deductions—Most items in this category are deductible only if your combined expenses exceed 2 percent of your AGI. Following is a list of the

fast fact

You may deduct allowable interest payments only if you are legally obligated to repay the underlying loan.

**smart
step**

Keep track of your auto mileage and out-of-pocket expenses while you perform charitable services. The mileage is deductible at 14 cents per mile, and the out-of-pocket expenses are generally deductible as well.

most common miscellaneous itemized deductions that are subject, in their sum, to the 2 percent threshold.

- **Employee business expenses such as transportation, travel, gifts, and entertainment necessary to your job and that you pay yourself** (You will probably need Form 2106, Employee Business Expenses to calculate your deduction for this type of expense)
- **Expenses you pay tax professionals, the cost of tax software, and online tax preparation expenses that help you determine your tax liability**
- **Investment expenses such as fees paid for investment advice, the rental of a safe deposit box if the box contains bonds or other securities, and appraisal fees, among others**
- **Job-seeking expenses for a job in your current occupation**

As you did with medical expenses, toward the end of the year check how close you are to the minimum threshold. If it looks like you'll fall short, hold off paying qualified expenses until next year. If it looks like you'll exceed the minimum threshold, pay more of your qualified expenses to increase your deduction.

Some miscellaneous itemized deductions are *not* subject to the 2 percent threshold. Here's a partial list of fully deductible items:

- **Casualty and theft losses from income-producing property**
- **Gambling losses, to the extent of gambling winnings reported as taxable income on line 21, Form 1040**
- **Impairment-related work expenses** (for example, the cost of an interpreter for a deaf person, assuming he or she pays the interpreter)

THE CHALLENGE

Rita was overjoyed. She had always dreamed of owning her own home and had finally saved enough money for the down payment on the house of her dreams. She purchased her new home in October and paid $1,000 in points to obtain her loan. The points qualified to be deducted on her current year tax return. Rita's mortgage was for thirty years and she began making her loan payments in November.

Fast-forward to tax season and we find Rita confused by the deductible points and interest that are shown on the Form 1098 she received from her mortgage company. "Everyone told me that it would pay for me to own my own home because I would finally be able to itemize my deductions, but it looks like I still don't have enough," said Rita.

THE PLAN

Rita visited her tax professional, who helped her understand what was happening with her tax situation. Even when Rita added to her deductions the $1,000 she had paid in points to close her loan, her standard deduction still exceeded her itemized deductions. This was because Rita purchased her home late in the year and had not incurred a significant amount of mortgage interest expense to deduct.

Rita understood these reasons, but was still concerned that she would lose the value of the $1,000 in points she had paid. Her tax professional explained that she could still deduct the points, but that it would be over the lifetime of the loan. He pointed out that for this year, Rita's standard deduction exceeds her itemized deductions, but that next year she will probably itemize.

Juggling Your Itemized Deductions

If your itemized deductions are close to the standard deduction year after year, you may be able to do a little planning, juggle some expenses, and itemize your deductions every other year. Before the end of year, make an accurate estimate of your itemized deductions to determine if they will exceed the standard deduction. If not, postpone paying deductible expenses until the next year when they may have some additional value. If your estimate shows that your itemized deductions will exceed the standard deduction, pay as many additional deductible expenses as you can before year-end. Every additional deductible expense that you pay before the end of the year will increase your total deductions and lower your tax bill.

Using Tax Credits to Your Advantage

What is a tax credit? Basically, a tax credit will lower your tax bill dollar-for-dollar, whereas a deduction will only lower your tax bill by a fraction of the deductible amount. Here's an example: A tax credit of $1,000 reduces your tax liability by $1,000 while a tax deduction of $1,000 saves you only $270 if your marginal tax rate is 27 percent.

Listed below are a few common tax credits available to taxpayers:

Child-Related Credits—There are three main credits relating to children: the child and dependent care credit; the child tax credit; and the child adoption credit. Not only did the 2001 tax law increase the child tax credit to $600, but it also relaxed the guidelines for claiming the refundable additional tax credit. The maximum tax credit for adoption was increased to $10,000 for expenses paid after 2001, regardless of whether the child is considered a special-needs child. The allowable income level at which the adoption credit begins to be phased out has been increased to $150,000. For more information about the valuable child-related credits, See IRS Publication 17, Your Federal Income Tax.

Earned Income Credit—The earned income credit (EIC) can lower your taxes substantially. If your earned income and adjusted gross income are less than $34,178 for 2002, you may be able to claim this credit. Recall that the EIC is a refundable credit. That means that you get it even if your tax was reduced to zero.

Education Tax Credits—The two tax credits for higher education are the Hope credit and the lifetime learning credit. The Hope credit, of up to $1,500 annually per eligible student, is tailored for expenses incurred in the first two years of college. The lifetime learning credit applies to tuition costs for undergraduates, graduates, and those improving job skills through a training program. We'll cover these credits in more detail in Chapter 9.

Foreign Tax Credit—This credit eases double taxation on United States taxpayers who pay income taxes to a foreign country or a United States possession and to the United States on the same income. You have the choice either to deduct the foreign income tax as an itemized deduction on Schedule A, or to claim this credit. Generally, claiming the credit is more advantageous because it offsets your tax liability dollar-for-dollar.

Retirement Savings Contributions Credit—New for 2002 is the saver's credit. This tax credit is based on the first $2,000 contributed to IRAs, 401(k)s, and certain other retirement plans. The saver's credit can be claimed in addition to the deduction for traditional IRA contributions and the exclusion for elective deferrals. Income limits apply. Form 8880 and its instructions provide complete information about this credit.

fast fact

For 2002, the maximum adoption tax credit is $10,000 of qualified expenses per adoption, up from $5,000 ($6,000 for a special-needs child) for 2001.

The cost of education that helps you retain or improve your skills in your present occupation may be deductible or eligible for the lifetime learning credit.

Often-Overlooked Tax Deductions

When it comes to taxes, we've seen just about everything. One thing we see more of than we'd like is deductions that taxpayers miss—time and time again. Here are some commonly overlooked tax deductions. We hope they're not overlooked anymore:

Charitable Contributions Made through Payroll Deductions—If you have charitable contributions deducted from your paycheck, you may forget about them at tax time because you didn't write a check. Be sure to include them when your return is prepared.

Cost of Tax Preparation—Tax return preparation fees, including the cost of tax preparation software, and online tax preparation expenses are deductible as miscellaneous itemized deductions for the year that you paid the costs.

Home-Office Deduction—If you use a qualified home office regularly and exclusively for your business needs and meet several other requirements, you can claim a deduction. There's much more on home office tax issues in Chapter 8.

Job-Seeking Expenses—If you are looking for a different job in the same field in which you are employed (or were recently employed), you can deduct job-seeking expenses, including your ordinary and necessary travel expenses away from home while you look for work. You can take this deduction even if you don't land a new job.

Personal Property Taxes—Taxes you pay on personal property, such as a vehicle, may be deductible. The tax is deductible if it is based on the value of the property and not something else such as weight or horsepower. The tax must also be charged on an annual basis, even if the tax is collected more or less than once a year.

Points on Mortgages—When you refinance or otherwise pay off your mortgage, you may deduct in full the balance of points you have been deducting over the life of the mortgage.

State Tax Return Check-Offs—Many states have charitable check-off items on the state income tax return. By marking certain boxes on the return, you can donate part of your refund to various causes such as the preservation of wildlife or the protection of abused children. Check your previous year's state return for these deductible donations.

Qualified Work-Related Transportation Expenses—If you keep good records, you generally can claim a mileage allowance or your actual expenses for business use of the vehicle, plus parking and tolls.

Value of Donated Goods—The value (or cost, if less) of household goods and personal effects given to a charitable organization is tax deductible. Many people underestimate the value of their donations to charity.

These are just a few deductions that can escape your attention. There are many more that the rest of this book and/or your tax professional can help you find.

fast fact

The cost of gas and oil (or a standard mileage allowance), parking, tolls, or bus and taxi fares, to obtain medical care or perform volunteer work for a charity are tax deductible.

the ESSENTIALS

1 A deduction reduces income that would otherwise be subject to tax.

2 Every dollar by which deductions, exemptions, and credits reduce your tax helps keep more money in your pocket.

3

Figure your itemized deductions on Schedule A to determine if you should itemize or not. You may elect to claim the standard deduction or itemize deductions, whichever is more beneficial.

4

Tax credits are especially valuable because they reduce your tax liability dollar-for-dollar.

6 [ON MAIN STREET: How Taxes Affect Your Investments]

"Don't tax you, don't tax me, tax that fellow behind the tree."
—Former Senator Russell Long

Capital loss in excess of capital gain can be written off against ordinary income up to $3,000 per year. Any remaining net capital loss may be carried into future years.

Wall Street has long been a symbol of wealth, or at least the potential to create it. For decades, fortunes can be made and lost each time Wall Street's closing bell rings. We may have not yet made our fortunes, but what goes up and down on this famous street tends to have an impact on all of us. As the value of individual stocks, bonds, and other securities rises and falls, the prices of the things that they affect change as well. This includes everything from the price of a gallon of gasoline to the value of your retirement nest egg. Most of us have investments, whether or not we think of them that way.

Tax laws have a tremendous effect on your investments. Did you realize a gain on the sale of a stock? Great, but don't count your profits just yet, because there are tax consequences as well. Did the bear market catch you in the wrong position and you sold for a loss? Too bad, but is a loss all bad news? Not necessarily, because the loss may actually help you reduce your tax liability. Sound confusing or too taxing to discuss? It doesn't have to be.

As we've discussed throughout the book, there is a lot you can do to influence your tax situation and get the results you want. When it comes to your investments, the process is no different. First, you need to understand what types of investment taxes there are, such as capital gains and early withdrawal penalties, and the basics of how they work. Then it's up to you and your tax professional to craft a sound tax strategy that will allow you to maximize the value of your investments.

Your Investments and How They Are Taxed

These days, it seems as though you can be taxed on just about anything, and your investments are no different. It doesn't matter if you put your money in a simple passbook savings account or invest in government bonds or mutual funds; there will inevitably be tax consequences, some in your favor, some not. Sooner or later, the tax bill will also come due on your tax-deferred investments such as 401(k) plans and IRAs, which we'll cover in the next chapter. Your house, a big investment in itself, may also be affected by the tax code.

Investment income in the form of interest, dividends, and capital gains is usually (but not always) taxable.

Interest—Most interest income from your investments is taxable. Note, however, that municipal bond interest escapes federal tax and may escape state tax as well. Interest on federal obligations, such as savings bond interest, is taxable on your federal return, but not on your state return.

The interest you paid on investment-related loans may be deductible as an itemized deduction. Your deduction is limited to your investment income. Any excess interest expense you have may be carried over to future years. You may elect to include a long-term capital gain in your investment income for determining the investment interest deduction. But making the election requires that you forego the lower capital gains rates for these gains. Your tax professional can help you determine which option is better for you.

Dividends—Dividends represent the payout to shareholders for a portion of the profits of the organization paying the dividends. Shareholders generally receive the dividends in cash or may be able to reinvest them through a dividend reinvestment plan.

Dividends come in three varieties. Ordinary dividends are taxable. Capital gain distributions are taxable as long-term capital gains. Nontaxable distributions are just that: nontaxable. They represent a return of your investment and decrease the basis of your investment. Form 1099-DIV has separate boxes for each type of dividend.

Capital gains and losses—When you sell investment property (which can be any number of things, including shares of stock, bonds, shares of a mutual fund, or certain real estate) at a profit, a capital gain is generated. Conversely, when you sell at a loss, a capital loss is generated.

If your sale generated a capital gain, the **holding period** of the asset helps determine the tax treatment it receives. Capital gains and losses are long-term if the property sold was held for more than one year and short-term if the property sold was held for one year or less. If, after combining all capital gains and losses, you have a net short-term gain, the gain is taxed at your marginal tax rate. If the net result is a long-term gain, the maximum rate varies (8, 10, or 20 percent) with your tax bracket. If your capital losses exceed your capital gains, you can deduct up to $3,000 of the net loss from your other income. The amount in excess of $3,000 can be carried to future years.

The above description of the taxation of capital gains and losses fits the majority of capital transactions. However, you need to be aware that special rules apply to the sale of collectibles, qualified small business stock, certain depreciable real property, and qualified property you have held for more than five years. The complexity of the tax picture for capital gains and losses is a good topic to review with your tax professional.

Creating an Investment Tax-Planning Strategy

The goal of your investment plan is almost certainly to maximize your wealth. Working hand-in-hand with your investment plan, the goal of your investment tax plan should be to help you minimize your tax liability. Once your plan is in place, you'll know when the time is right to take advan-

A holding period is the length of time you own an asset, such as a stock, bond, or mutual fund. More than one year is considered long–term and one year or less is considered short–term.

tage of some of the many tax-saving opportunities that occur throughout the year. You've probably heard of investors who attempt to time the market by purchasing stock when the price is low and selling stock when the price is high. Timing in tax planning is just as important. By not planning ahead, you could forget a key date and lose out on both an investment and a tax-saving opportunity. Plan ahead and you may be able to reduce your tax even if your investment strategy didn't turn out the way you thought it would.

Here's a quick example: If you sell capital assets (such as stocks, mutual fund shares, real estate, and bonds) during the year, you'll have a gain or a loss on each transaction. Near the end of the year, say in October or November, review your sales of capital assets to see if you have a net loss or gain from all your transactions.

If you have a net capital loss of more than $3,000 (the amount allowed against ordinary income), consider cashing in some investments that are currently showing paper gains. The reason? The losses you already have will offset your gains, thus, in effect, allowing you to realize capital gains while avoiding the tax you would otherwise pay.

If you have a large net gain, consider the opposite tactic: Sell some assets currently showing a paper loss. Again, your losses will offset your gains and reduce your tax bill.

This is great tax advice, but don't follow it blindly. Remember that tax savings are the icing on the cake. The main course is the financial soundness of the investment and how it fits in your long-range financial plan. So think about what you're considering selling before you do so just to reduce your tax bill.

fast fact

Investment-related income that is not taxable by the IRS includes life insurance proceeds received on the death of the insured and municipal bond interest.

More on Holding Periods

As we mentioned above, the amount of tax you owe when an investment is sold is based partially on the length of time you owned it, or the holding period. The gain or loss on the sale of the asset is calculated by comparing the asset's **basis** (your investment in it) with its selling price. The holding period—not the actual gain or loss—helps determine the rate at which the gain is taxed.

The holding period of property is measured in months, and you must own the property more than one year to receive long-term treatment on its sale. Do not count the day you bought the property, but count the day of sale. For example, if you purchase stock on July 1 and sell it the following July 1, the sale will be considered short-term because your holding period was not more than one year. If you wait until July 2 of the following year to sell your stock, the sale will receive long-term treatment. As you can see from this example, timing is important when forming a plan to minimize your tax liability.

Taxing Different Kinds of Investments

Let's take a look at how different types of investments are taxed.

Stocks—Here it comes again—the importance of good record keeping. Not only is it important to know which stocks you have bought, sold, and currently own, but it is also vital to be able to determine how any sales will be taxed. If you have made multiple purchases of a certain stock, such as 100 shares on July 1 and another 100 shares of the same stock on August 1, you'll need to keep track of each different basis and purchase date. When you decide to sell some of your stock, you'll need to determine which shares to sell. If you don't

plain talk

An asset's basis is your investment in it for tax purposes. In most cases, this is your cost. You may need to make certain adjustments to your basis before computing your gain or loss when disposing of an asset.

THE CHALLENGE

Ian, a single electrical engineer, made a good income, but he hadn't saved or invested much. "I was young and having a good time. I tended to spend all my money on sport cars and clothes," Ian explained. "I managed to save enough for a six-month emergency fund, but that was about all."

When Ian received an $8,000 bonus, he decided to invest it in a good stock. After doing some research, Ian chose a tech stock and invested the full amount in it. Ian monitored the stock's price every day, and the ups and downs of the market made him nervous. After eleven months, the stock's price was high enough that he could make a couple thousand dollars by selling it. "I decided to sell for two reasons," said Ian. "First, I could make a profit and, second, it made me nervous to watch the stock price every day."

THE PLAN

Incidentally, Ian had an appointment with his tax professional to discuss a tax issue and happened to mention his decision to sell his stock immediately. The tax professional, upon learning that Ian had owned the stock for eleven months, pointed out that if Ian sold the stock immediately, he would pay tax on the gain at his marginal rate, which in Ian's case was 35 percent. If Ian waited to sell until he had owned the stock for more than one year, the tax on his gain would be reduced to 20 percen. Of course, during this time the price of the stock could also change. The tax professional also referred Ian to a good financial advisor who could help him make a comprehensive investment plan that would take into account Ian's dislike of financial risk.

"My tax professional not only saved me a bunch of tax on my stock sale, but he helped me get started on a more responsible financial future," Ian reported.

decide, Uncle Sam will decide for you by applying the FIFO rule, an accounting term that means "first in first out." Why should you care as long as you get the price that you want? Well, determining which shares to sell and when could make a big difference in your tax bill.

Remember that the holding period helps to shape the tax treatment your sale will receive. If you held on to the asset for one year or less, it will be a short-term gain or loss and the gain, if any, will be taxed as ordinary income at your marginal rate. If you held on to the asset for more than one year, it will be a long-term gain or loss and generally receive more favorable tax treatment.

Let's build on our earlier example. You purchased the 100 shares of stock July 1 for $3,000 (including commission), giving you a basis of $30 per share. You purchased another 100 shares of the same stock August 1 for $4,000 (including commission), resulting in a basis of $40 per share.

Over the next year, the price of the stock rises to $50 per share and you decide to sell 100 shares on December 1 of the following year. If you simply tell your broker to sell 100 shares, it will be assumed (under the FIFO rule) that you sold the 100 shares you purchased in July ($30 per share basis) and you will wind up with a taxable gain of $20 per share, or $2,000. But if you specify which shares to sell and indicate the shares purchased on August 1 ($40 per share basis) instead, the taxable gain will be just $10 per share, or $1,000.

Either way, you wind up with $5,000, and the gain on the sale of the stock will enjoy the long-term capital gain rates (8 percent, 10 percent, or 20 percent) because both lots of stock were held for more than one year. If you choose the shares with the higher basis and your capital gains tax rate is 20 percent, your tax liability would be $200 versus $400 for the sale of the other shares.

Next, let's look at a few other investment situations where the timing can make a big difference in your tax liability.

Wash Sales—If you sell stocks or securities at a loss and then purchase, or acquire an option to purchase, substantially identical stocks or securities within thirty days before or after the sale, the wash sale rule applies. That doesn't mean that you are going to take a bath on the transaction; it simply means that the loss on a wash sale is not deductible. This rule was put into place to prevent taxpayers from selling stocks or securities to claim a capital loss and then buying the stock or security right back. Instead, the loss that is not deductible is added to the basis of the new stock or security. If you really want to be able to deduct the loss, leave a thirty-one-day window before or after the sale to repurchase the stock.

Short Sales—A short sale occurs when you borrow stock from your broker to sell because you expect the price of a stock to decline. You then replace the stock at a future date with identical stock that you own or stock that you purchased for that purpose. If the price of the stock declined as you expected, you'll have a gain. If you were wrong and the price increased, you'll have a loss. The tax rules concerning short sales are fairly complicated, so you'll want to discuss this matter with your financial or tax advisor, preferably before you engage in this type of transaction.

Last-Minute Sales—When you trade stocks and securities, it usually takes three business days from the day you sell until the day you actually get your money. This is referred to as settling. The time delay isn't usually important unless you really need the money. But settling around year-end is important. At year-end, the settlement period may actually start in one year and finish in the next. What does that mean to you? The tax code requires that a gain or loss must be reported on the tax return for the year in which the trade occurred, not the year in which it was settled. Any gains or losses on sales or exchanges up to and including those on December 31 must be reported on your current year's return.

smart step

If you finance the sale of your home to a buyer who uses it as a personal residence, make sure you obtain the Social Security number of the buyer. Failure to do so could result in a penalty from the IRS.

Installment Sales—Buy now, pay later—who hasn't heard of that before? In tax law there is a similar concept. An installment sale is the sale of real property or the casual sale of personal property at a gain if all or part of the sales price is to be received one or more years after the year of sale. The installment sale rules don't apply to publicly traded stock, but you may be able to make use of them if you sell some real or personal property for a gain. Say, for example, you sell the north forty acres of your farm to your neighbor, but he can't pay for it all at once. If your neighbor pays you over a number of years, you may report the gain each year instead of all at once at the time of the sale as you would have if he had paid you in full.

Keep in mind that the installment sales rules are optional. You are allowed to report the entire gain in the year of the sale. Usually, reporting the income over a period of years as you receive the payments is the tax-wise decision, but not always. For example, if you're in a low (or 0 percent) tax bracket this year and your gain would be taxed at an 8 percent, 10 percent, or 15 percent rate, you may want to go ahead and report the total gain. But also consider the value of keeping the money used to pay the tax for the life of the contract rather than paying it up front. If you have an installment gain, you'll want to discuss both options with your tax professional.

Mutual Funds—Mutual funds invest in stocks, bonds, or both, and sell shares of the fund to investors. Thus, a stock mutual fund and an individual stock may generate the same types of investment income: gain or loss from the sale of shares and dividend distributions. However, mutual funds typically have annual capital gain distributions, and fund investors commonly reinvest their capital gain and dividend distributions.

When you sell mutual fund shares, any gain on the sale will be subject to capital gains taxes. You can also deduct a loss on the sale of mutual fund shares that have declined in value. The amount of gain or loss is the difference between the basis of the fund shares you sold and the selling price. You may elect to use an average basis method for computing the basis of your mutual fund shares. Some funds compute the average basis for you. See IRS Publication 564 for details.

Dividend distributions from mutual funds are mainly from interest and dividends earned by the fund from investments. Capital gain distributions consist of the net long-term capital gain the mutual fund realized from sales of securities during the year. They must be reported as income on your tax return whether your receive them in cash or automatically reinvest them. Happily, any portion of dividends identified as municipal bond interest is reported as tax-exempt interest, and capital gain distributions are taxed at the capital gains tax rates, often lower than your marginal tax rate (normally 8 percent, 10 percent, or 20 percent).

Municipal Bonds—Interest on bonds or other obligations of a state or political subdivision of a state is exempt from federal income tax. These obligations are generally known as municipal bonds or "muni-bonds." Interest on qualified bonds may be free of state income taxes for residents of the issuing state. The rate of interest earned is typically lower than for taxable bonds, but municipal bonds' tax-exempt status helps to make up the difference through tax savings. Be aware that if you sell the bond, you will incur a capital gain or loss that must be reported on your income tax return.

fast fact

You may be able to claim a foreign tax credit if you own shares in a mutual fund that invests in foreign securities. The credit is almost always worth more than an itemized deduction because it offsets your tax liability dollar-for-dollar.

While tax-free interest may be attractive, it may not always be the best investment. Use the following chart to see comparable yields for taxable and nontaxable investments.

TAX-EXEMPT VS. TAXABLE YIELDS						
TAX BRACKET	10%	15%	27%	30%	35%	38.6%
TAX-EXEMPT YIELD (%)			TAXABLE YIELD (%)			
4.0	4.44	4.71	5.48	5.71	6.15	6.51
4.5	5.00	5.29	6.16	6.43	6.92	7.33
5.0	5.56	5.88	6.85	7.14	7.69	8.14
5.5	6.11	6.47	7.53	7.86	8.46	8.96
6.0	6.67	7.06	8.22	8.57	9.23	9.77
6.5	7.22	7.65	8.90	9.29	10.00	10.59
7.0	7.78	8.24	9.59	10.00	10.77	11.40
7.5	8.33	8.82	10.27	10.71	11.54	12.21
8.0	8.89	9.41	10.96	11.43	12.31	13.03
8.5	9.44	10.00	11.64	12.14	13.08	13.84
9.0	10.00	10.59	12.33	12.86	13.85	14.66

How to use this chart: Find the line that shows the rate of interest you can receive on a tax-exempt bond. Then find the column that shows your tax bracket. The percentage shown is the interest rate you would need to receive on a taxable bond to have the same after-federal-tax yield as with the tax-exempt bond.

Example: If you're in the 27 percent bracket and you can earn 6 percent on a tax-exempt bond, you should not purchase a taxable bond unless the rate exceeds 8.22 percent.

Source: H&R Block

Life Insurance—Life insurance can be a worthwhile investment as well as protection for heirs in the event of the insured's death. Some policies combine investments with insurance and also enjoy tax-favored status. These tax-favored policies include universal life, whole life, and single-premium life. The tax bill on earnings and increased value on most life insurance policies is deferred until you cash in the policy. Proceeds are generally not taxable if the policy has been cashed either because of a terminal illness of the insured, or to pay for qualified long-term care due to chronic illness of the insured. If the policy is in force when you die, the proceeds go to your beneficiary completely free of income tax.

Should a policyholder choose, he or she may be able to access the earnings inside the policy prior to his or her death. A policyholder may be able to obtain a loan against the cash value in the policy. If the loan is not paid back prior to death, the outstanding amount is deducted from the death benefit.

Consult with your insurance professional and your tax professional before investing. A life insurance policy must meet certain criteria to be classified as life insurance for tax benefits. If it doesn't, all earnings are taxable to the insured each year as earned and credited to the policy, or in the first year the policy fails to meet the criteria.

Annuities—An annuity is a contract that is usually issued by an insurance company. Earnings in an annuity grow tax-deferred until they are withdrawn, either in a lump sum or by annuitizing (yes, that's a real word) the contract. *Annuitizing* means the insurance company makes payments to you over a fixed period of time, for your life, or for your life and after you die, to your survivor. Some annuities guarantee you will receive no less than your investment. Depending on the type of the annuity you invest in, you may be given choices as to what kinds of investments the return on your annuity will be linked.

fast
fact

A portion of life insurance premiums may go into investments that build cash value. Earnings on the cash value are not taxed until the policy is cashed in.

95

An annuity contract is valuable because tax on investment earnings is deferred until the earnings are distributed to you. This benefit is similar to other plans such as a 401(k) or an individual retirement arrangement (IRA). Unlike a 401(k) or traditional IRA, you can't deduct your premiums or exclude them from income. And, of course, annuities don't have the advantage of totally tax-free withdrawals offered by a Roth IRA. But each distribution you receive will be partially tax-free based on the ratio of how much you invested to how much you can expect to receive. If you withdraw any of your money before age fifty-nine and a half, you'll probably have to pay a 10 percent penalty tax. (There are some exceptions.)

Are Investment-Related Expenses Tax Deductible?

Many expenses related to investments that produce taxable income are tax deductible. However, any expenses related to tax-exempt investments cannot be deducted.

Here is a short list of deductible investment expenses. These expenses are deductible as miscellaneous itemized deductions if your total miscellaneous itemized deductions exceed 2 percent of your AGI.

- **Depreciation on a home computer used for investment activities** (limited, and keep a time and task log)
- **Fees for online trading** (restricted to account maintenance-related fees)
- **Investment club operating expenses** (your share)
- **Investment fees, custodial fees, trust administration fees, and other expenses you paid that are necessary to collect investment income or maintain your taxable investments**
- **IRA fees billed and paid separately from your IRA contribution**
- **Safe-deposit box rental if the box is used to store stocks, bonds, or investment documents**
- **Subscriptions to investment magazines and newsletters**

Remember, trading fees and commissions for buying or selling an asset are not deductible; instead they increase your basis and thus reduce your gain or increase your loss when you sell or otherwise dispose of the asset.

Taxes and Your Home

Home ownership has long been considered a part of the American dream. A piece of land with a home to call your own, a place to sink roots and become part of a community—sounds pretty good, doesn't it? In addition to these good social reasons, owning a home can be a smart investment and one that comes with many tax-saving opportunities. Like any other investment, a home's value can rise and fall; however, over time, home ownership has been an excellent investment for many people. For some people, their home may be their biggest single investment.

If you buy a home, not only will you get the joy of home ownership, but you may also be able to get the joy of reducing your tax liability by deducting home ownership-related expenses such as points, mortgage loan interest, and real estate taxes. Here are the basic tax-saving elements of home ownership:

Interest—When you pay interest on a qualified home mortgage, you may generally deduct the interest in full on Schedule A. The mortgage must be secured by your principal residence or a second residence. For income tax purposes, a principal residence is the one where you live and return to after short absences. You can have only one principal residence at a time. A second residence is one that is only used for personal purposes or, if rented, then used for personal purposes for no more than the greater of fourteen days or 10 percent of the number of days you rent the home at fair rental value. If you own more than two homes, you may claim the interest deduction on only one as a second residence for any given year.

You may qualify to exclude up to $250,000 ($500,000 if married and filing jointly) of gain from the sale or exchange of your main home. To qualify, you generally must have owned and lived in the home for a total of two out of the five years immediately preceding the date of the sale.

Points—Loan fees that you pay solely for the use of the money are often referred to as points. The points you pay are deductible in full in the year paid as an itemized deduction on Schedule A if certain conditions are met. To qualify, the loan has to be for the purchase or improvement of, and be secured by, your principal residence. Charging of points must be an established practice in your area, and the amount of points cannot be excessive. The amount must be computed as a percentage of the stated principal amount of the mortgage. Finally, the amount you paid at or before closing, plus any points the seller paid, must be at least as much as the points charged.

If you cannot itemize in the year you purchase the home, but will be able to itemize in later years, it's to your advantage to elect to deduct the points over the life of the loan. If you refinance the loan or sell the home before you pay off the loan, you can deduct any remaining points in the year of refinancing or sale.

Home Equity Credit Lines—These are popular sources for obtaining a fast and convenient loan complete with tax-saving features. Because the debt is secured by your home, interest on the loan is deductible, subject to certain limitations. You may be able to trade nondeductible debt (such as a large credit card balance or vehicle loan) for debt that is deductible. While certainly a tax advantage, never take out a home equity loan unless you are certain you can make the payments. If you fail to repay the loan, one of your most valuable possessions, your home, may be at risk.

Rental Property

Ordinary and necessary expenses incurred in connection with rental property are deductible. These include items such as advertising, commissions to brokers, reasonable compensation you pay to others in connection with the property, and insurance premiums. Repairs that are ordinary and necessary to maintain the property in a safe, rentable condition and that do not increase the value or prolong the life of the property are also deductible in full. Depending on your tax situation, you may want to consider making repairs or paying for deductible expenses in December rather than January. Doing so will help decrease your taxable income or increase your loss.

Another tax benefit of owning rental property is the potential to use up to $25,000 of losses from your rental property to offset other income. To qualify, you must actively manage the property. If your modified adjusted gross income is $100,000 or less, you can claim the full allowance; if over this amount, your allowance will be limited; the $25,000 limit is reduced by $1 for each $2 by which your modified adjusted gross income exceeds $100,000.

This Old Vacation House

So you own a vacation home? Lucky you! If you offer it for rent, you may be able to claim some tax deductions too.

How you report income and deductions for the rental of a vacation home (or other personal-use dwelling unit) depends on how many days during the year the unit is rented at fair rental value, how many days you or someone related to you uses the unit, and whether you are using the dwelling unit as a residence. If you use your vacation home for more than the greater of fourteen days or 10

smart step

See your tax professional before you take out a home-equity loan or establish a line of credit secured by your home. He or she can help you determine what portion of your interest payments will be deductible.

smart step

Rent out our vacation home for up to fourteen days a year and pocket the money tax-free. The mortgage interest (if the house is a qualified second residence) and real estate taxes are deductible in full, but no other rental expenses are deductible.

percent of the number of days it is rented at fair rental value, the house is considered a personal-use dwelling. If so, your rental expense deductions are limited to the amount of your rental income. However, if you are able to limit the personal use of your vacation home, it may be classified as a rental property. If your vacation home qualifies as a rental property, you may be able to deduct losses as discussed under rental property.

Ultimately, taxes play a role in the overall value you realize from your investments. Consider the tax implications of your different investments and plan wisely, but remember the most important thing is to make sure you have a sound investment plan to help you realize your goals. Your financial advisor can prove to be a valuable resource in that regard.

the ESSENTIALS

1 The goal of your investment plan is almost certainly to maximize your wealth. The goal of your investment tax plan should be to help you minimize your tax liability on these investments.

2 Investment income generally consists of interest, dividends, and capital gains.

3 The timing of the purchase and sale of your investments helps determine the tax treatment they will receive and the amount of your tax liability.

4 Home ownership is an investment that has many tax advantages.

7 [PLAN NOW, PLAY LATER:

Tax Planning and Your
Retirement
]

"In retirement, only money and symptoms are consequential."
—Mason Cooley

What are your retirement plans? Do they include leading a carefree life of leisure, spending time with the grandkids, or taking that trip to Tahiti you've always promised yourself? All of these dreams sound pretty good, but the plans you make today, and actually implement, are most likely going to shape the quality of your retirement. That's why you need to take advantage of as many tax-favored (tax-free and tax-deferred) investments as possible.

In **tax-favored** plans, your earnings grow tax-deferred. You won't pay taxes on the investment earnings until you withdraw them. One plan, the Roth IRA, allows you to withdraw your money completely tax-free as long as you keep your hands off it until you turn fifty-nine and a half and have been invested in the Roth IRA for at least five full years. Some plans help you reduce your tax liability today by reducing your taxable income or qualifying you for a deduction and/or a credit. There are many great choices out there and it's up to you to take advantage of them to fulfill your retirement dreams.

plain talk

With a tax-favored investment, the earnings (interest, dividends, and capital gains) are not taxed until withdrawn.

Tax-Wise Saving For Retirement

Hopefully, saving for retirement is one of your main financial goals. The tax code provides several tax-favored retirement plan options. A common feature of these options is that the earnings grow tax-deferred year to year. That's important over time because it allows the earnings to compound at a higher effective rate. Below, we've offered a general description of some of the more common tax-favored plans. Before we get to that, however, here are three general retirement planning principles you might find useful.

- **It's never too early—and often not too late—to start.** The sooner you put money away, the more time it has to grow.
- **Retirement tax planning is important enough and complicated enough that you should consider meeting with a financial advisor who can help**

you tailor a personalized plan. The information we provide here will help you have a more informed discussion with your advisor.

- **Unless you're approaching age fifty-nine and a half, consider money invested in a tax-favored retirement plan to be a long-term investment.** If you withdraw money from the plan before then, you'll usually pay a penalty. If you can't wait until retirement to access the money, it's probably better to choose another investment such as a municipal bond fund or an investment earning taxable returns.

Now let's take a look at the various options for planning a tax-wise retirement.

Individual Retirement Arrangements (IRAs)

Investing in an IRA can be a good idea, even if your contributions aren't deductible. The maximum contribution for 2002 is $3,000 (plus an extra $500 if you're age fifty or older). The earnings in your IRA will grow tax-deferred until you decide to withdraw them. If you invest in a traditional IRA, you may be able to deduct all or a portion of your contributions.

If you are a single taxpayer and participate in an employer-maintained retirement plan, you can deduct the full amount of your allowable contributions to a traditional IRA if your **modified adjusted gross income** (MAGI) for 2002 is $34,000 or less. If your MAGI is above this amount, the deduction will be limited. The deduction disappears completely if your MAGI is $44,000 or more. If you do not participate in an employer-maintained retirement plan, you can deduct all your allowable contributions, regardless of your MAGI.

Married taxpayers filing jointly are subject to more complex rules. If neither spouse participates in an employer-maintained retirement plan, allowable contributions to a traditional IRA are fully deductible. If both participate in an employer-maintained retirement plan, allowable contributions are fully deductible if the

plain talk

Modified adjusted gross income (MAGI) is the sum of your adjusted gross income, plus certain tax-favored items you deducted or excluded. These items will vary depending on how the MAGI computation is applied.

couples' MAGI is $54,000 or less, partly deductible if over this amount, and non-deductible if their MAGI is $64,000 or more. If your spouse participates in an employer-maintained retirement plan but you don't, only your allowable contributions to a traditional IRA are fully deductible if your MAGI is $150,000 or less, partly deductible if over this amount, and nondeductible if your MAGI is $160,000 or more.

Withdrawals from traditional IRAs are taxable (unless you made nondeductible contributions, in which case a portion of each withdrawal will be nontaxable). During the year you reach age seventy and a half, you must begin making withdrawals from your traditional IRA. You may postpone this required withdrawal until April 1 of the following year if you want to lower your taxable income for the current year. Be aware that you must make a second withdrawal by December 31 of the following year. This could result in your paying more tax for any of the following reasons: your increased income puts you in a higher marginal tax bracket; more of your Social Security benefits become taxable; and deductions and credits subject to an AGI limit will be further reduced.

Roth IRAs

A Roth IRA differs from a traditional IRA in several ways: Contributions to a Roth IRA are never deductible; qualified distributions (both contributions and earnings) are entirely tax-free if you take them at least five full years after you first established a Roth IRA *and* after you reach fifty-nine and a half; and you don't have to take distributions from a Roth IRA when you reach age seventy and a half.

Nonqualified distributions (generally those before age fifty-nine and a half) first come from amounts that have already been taxed, so a distribution may not be taxable. Generally, distributions from traditional IRAs are partially or fully taxable.

If you're eligible for both a deductible traditional IRA and a Roth IRA, your choice can be a difficult one. You'll need to balance your need for current deductions with your desire for tax-free retirement income.

Qualified Retirement Plan Penalties

The taxable portion of any early distribution (generally a distribution before you reach age fifty-nine and a half) from a qualified retirement plan is usually subject to a 10 percent penalty tax. Early distributions from the following types of plans are subject to the penalty: qualified pension, profit sharing, stock bonus, and employee annuity plans; tax-sheltered annuity plans; and traditional IRAs. Certain distributions from Roth IRAs and section 457 plans may also be subject to the penalty.

There are exceptions to the 10 percent penalty on early distributions from qualified plans. Common exceptions include:

- **Distributions on account of death or disability**
- **Distributions from an IRA to purchase a first home** (limited to $10,000)
- **Substantially equal distributions based on your life expectancy, received at least annually**
- **Higher education expenses** (IRAs only)
- **Distributions paid during or after the year you leave your job after attaining age fifty-five** (employer plans only)

Specific conditions apply to each of the above exceptions. There are more exceptions, but the requirements may be complicated. This is a subject to be discussed with your tax professional.

401(k) Plans

A section 401(k) plan is a qualified retirement plan in which an employee may elect to contribute a portion of his or her wages to the plan, which also reduces his or her taxable salary by the amount contributed. These contributions are tax-deferred until they are withdrawn. In addition, the investment income on these deferrals grows tax-deferred until it is withdrawn. Investors may often choose from a wide variety of investment options to match the investor's goals and preferences.

As with other investment choices for retirement, the better your knowledge of your options, the better able you will be to make informed choices. For 2002, the limit on contributions is $11,000, and the allowable limit increases in $1,000 annual increments until it reaches $15,000 in 2006. Workers age fifty or older by the end of the year may make "catch up" contributions of $1,000 above the normal limit. The "catch up" amount will increase in $1,000 annual increments until it reaches $5,000 in 2006.

When you participate in a 401(k) plan, your ability to deduct contributions to a traditional IRA may be limited. But, participating in a 401(k) plan may actually help you increase the size of your allowable IRA deduction. How? Because as your 401(k) plan contribution reduces your taxable wages your MAGI may be reduced so that a partial deduction may be allowable.

Generally, contributions to a 401(k) plan are difficult to access prior to retirement. You must prove that you have a financial need that is serious and urgent that cannot be met with other reasonably available resources, including a loan from your 401(k). The bottom line: In general, you must first use up your savings and exhaust your credit sources. It's up to your plan administrator to decide whether or not to permit hardship withdrawals, which of the allowable circumstances to cover, and whether you qualify.

If your hardship distribution is approved, there are still tax-related issues with which to contend. Hardship withdrawals are subject to income tax, and if you received the money before you reached age fifty-nine and a half, you'll have to meet an exception to avoid the 10 percent early-distribution penalty. The maximum distribution for hardship expenses is the total of your personal contributions to the account. You are not allowed to withdraw company deposits or investment earnings.

403(b) Plans

Employees of public schools and certain tax-exempt organizations are eligible to participate in tax-sheltered annuity (TSA) plans, also known as 403(b) plans. Eligible employers include nonprofit or charitable organizations and other public interest-oriented organizations, such as universities. There are two basic types of plans. Under one, the employer contributes to the TSA, and under the other, employees agree to a reduction in salary or they forgo a salary increase in return for the employer's contribution to the TSA. The tax advantages of a 403(b) plan are similar to those of a 401(k) plan with contributions and investment earnings growing tax-deferred until withdrawn.

fast fact

There are three big advantages to 401(k) plans: your contributions to the plan are pretax, many companies match a portion of the funds employees contribute, and earnings grow on a tax-deferred basis.

Retirement Plans for the Self-Employed

So, you took the plunge and became self-employed—and now you're the boss. Congratulations! Some people find there's nothing like the satisfaction of working for themselves. You call all the shots, but you also have all the responsibility. Not to add to your workload, but you also have the responsibility of planning for and funding your own retirement. Fortunately, you have some tax-favored options to help you (and your employees, if you have any).

As a self-employed person, you may establish a qualified retirement plan and deduct your payments to the plan. (In the past, these accounts were referred to as Keogh plans.) Your investment earnings will grow tax-free until they are withdrawn. Another feature of qualified plans is that you may establish and deduct your contributions to the plan even if you hold another job and are covered under your employer's qualified plan.

Defined Contribution and Defined Benefit Plans—These are the two basic types of qualified self-employed retirement plans. A defined contribution plan provides a separate account for each person covered by the plan, and benefits are based on the amount contributed to and accumulated in the plan. Two examples of defined contribution plans are profit sharing plans and 401(k) plans. A defined benefit plan provides for a set benefit and is any plan that is not a defined contribution plan. Most pension plans are defined benefit plans. Contributions to a defined benefit plan are based on what is necessary to achieve a specific benefit.

Simplified Employee Pension (SEP)—An SEP provides an easy way for you to contribute to your (and your employees', if any) retirement by setting up an individual retirement arrangement (IRA) for all eligible employees. The requirements for establishing an SEP are similar to the requirements for other qualified plans, but the rules are simpler (as the name implies). You may establish an SEP

CONTRIBUTIONS TO SELF-EMPLOYED RETIREMENT PLANS

	SEP-IRA	QUALIFIED SELF-EMPLOYED RETIREMENT PLANS	
Last Date for Contribution	Due date of your return, plus extensions	Due date of your return plus extensions. A new plan must be set up by December 31 of the year for which the contributions will be made.	
		DEFINED CONTRIBUTION PLANS	
Maximum Contribution	**Employee:** Smaller of $40,000 or 25 percent of participant's compensation[3]	For Your Employees	For Yourself as a Self-Employed Individual
		Money Purchase Smaller of $40,000 or 25 percent of employee's compensation[3]	**Money Purchase** Smaller of $40,000 or 20 percent of your net earnings[2]
	Self-employed: Smaller of $40,000 or 20 percent[2] of your net earnings[3]	**Profit Sharing** Smaller of $40,000 or 25 percent of employee's compensation[3]	**Profit Sharing** Smaller of $40,000 or 20 percent of your net earnings
		DEFINED BENEFIT PLANS	
		Amount needed to provide an annual retirement benefit no larger than the smaller of $160,000 or 100 percent of the participant's highest average compensation for three consecutive years.	
Time Limit to Begin Distributions[1]	April 1 of year after year you reach age $70\frac{1}{2}$	**For employees:** April 1 of the year after you reach age $70\frac{1}{2}$ or retire, whichever occurs later. **For self-employed individuals:** April 1 of the year after you reach age $70\frac{1}{2}$.	

[1] Distribution of at least the required minimum amount must be made each year if the entire balance is not distributed.

[2] 20 percent of the self-employed participant's net earnings after deducting this contribution.

[3] No more than $200,000 of compensation or net earnings may be taken into account.

Source: H&R Block

A SIMPLE plan can take the form of an IRA or a 401(k) plan.

even if you don't have employees. An annual contribution to an SEP is not required, but if a contribution is made, one must be made to every eligible employee's account based on the same percentage of his or her total compensation.

Savings Incentive Match Plan for Employees (SIMPLE)—Self-employed individuals and small employers may set up a SIMPLE plan as a 401(k) plan or as a traditional IRA for each employee who qualifies. Employee contributions must be based on a percentage of compensation and cannot exceed an annually set limit. The employer must match each employee's contribution on a dollar-for-dollar basis up to certain limitations and make a contribution for each eligible employee whether or not the employee contributes. Contributions to a SIMPLE plan are excluded from the employee's income and are tax-deferred. Distributions are taxed under the rules for traditional IRA distributions.

The Rules—Generally, you can contribute up to $40,000 to a defined contribution plan or SEP, or up to $7,000 to a SIMPLE plan. In addition to these limits, profit sharing and SEP plan contributions are also limited to a percentage of self-employment income. SIMPLE plans generally must be opened by October 1, and qualified plans must be opened by December 31 in order to deduct contributions for the current year, while an SEP can be opened on or before April 15. Contributions to these plans can be made as late as April 15 (or later, if you get an extension, by the due date of your return) in order to qualify as an adjustment for the previous tax year.

THE CHALLENGE

After years of spending their summer vacation at the beach, Ray and Sue had finally made the decision to move there permanently. After months of beachcombing for that perfect hideaway, they finally found their dream home right on the shore of the Gulf of Mexico. The only problem? The house cost $40,000 more than they'd planned to spend. To make matters worse, their real estate agent called to let them know that there were two other couples seriously interested in the property. They knew that they needed to come up with the money soon, or their dream house would be gone.

"I called my brother Orville," said Sue. "He agreed to lend us half, but we really didn't want to get involved with owing a family member money, and we still didn't know where to get the other half. Since there were two other couples interested in buying the house, the owners weren't willing to negotiate. I knew that I had to find the money because I wasn't about to let someone else buy our dream house."

THE PLAN

"My friend Linda in the benefits department at work told me I could get the rest of the money by borrowing from my 401(k) plan. I had no idea that I could even do that," Sue said. After talking it over with Linda, Sue discovered that her company plan did allow employees to borrow money from their accounts. She learned that she could borrow no more than half the value of her account, up to a maximum loan of $50,000, and that the loan must be repaid within five years, unless the money was used to buy a principal residence.

Sue was able to withdraw some money from her account early without paying either income tax or the 10 percent early withdrawal penalty. "A loan from my 401(k) saved the day. We got the house, and we didn't even have to borrow any money from my brother," added Sue.

Have your em-
ployer send the
money from a
lump-sum
distribution
directly to your
rollover IRA
and avoid the
20 percent
withholding.

The Word on Withholding

When you receive payments from a company retirement plan or take distributions from a traditional IRA, you must decide whether or not to have tax withheld from the payments. If you elect to take the money without having taxes withheld, you can make estimated tax payments yourself. A tax professional can determine your estimated income and the amount of advance tax payments you need to make. Estimated tax is discussed later in Chapter 8.

If you want tax to be withheld, you must file a Form W-4P with the payer. Withholding on these payments can be a smart option. It's convenient and taken out each month before you miss having the money. It can also eliminate the hassle of making quarterly estimated tax payments.

When you retire, or if you quit or get laid off from your job, another withholding rule will affect you. If you receive a lump-sum payment, the administrator of the plan normally will automatically withhold 20 percent of the total account balance and send it to the IRS. If you do roll the money over to an IRA, you will be able to avoid the tax. But the IRS has the money, you don't owe the tax, and you can't get a refund until you file your tax return after the end of the year. What's more, the 20 percent that was withheld is part of your distribution, so you'll have to come up with other funds to make a complete rollover and avoid tax and penalty on the 20 percent. The solution? Instruct the plan administrator to send the money *directly* to your IRA custodian. That way, you never handle the money so there is no 20 percent withholding.

Retirement is an important topic and something that you should think about sooner rather than later. In order to have enough time to build a nest egg to fund the quality of retirement you want, it's best to start planning early to take advantage of as many tax-favored options as possible. It bears repeating that because this topic is both important and complicated, you should consider meeting with a financial advisor to make sure you'll get the most out of your plan.

the ESSENTIALS

1

Get an early start planning and investing for retirement.

2

Saving for retirement should be one of your main financial goals. Let your tax plan help you take advantage of as many tax-favored investments as possible.

3

Unless you are close to retirement, try to think of your retirement-related investments as long-term investments. Don't access the money early if at all possible.

4

Retirement tax planning is important and complicated enough to consider consulting a professional advisor.

8 [TAKING CARE OF BUSINESS: Tax-Saving Tips for the Self-Employed]

"Look after the pennies and the pounds will look after themselves."   —Andrew Carnegie

The son of a Scottish weaver, Andrew Carnegie rose to become the powerful head of U.S. Steel in the early 1900s. A reported story from his childhood reveals how his business instinct was keen from the time he was a young child.

One day at school, Carnegie's teacher asked him to recite a proverb from the Bible. Carnegie thought for a moment and repeated what his mother had taught him, "Look after the pennies and the pounds will look after themselves."

While his classmates may have laughed at him and his teacher may not have been too happy with his answer, Carnegie had already mastered an important lesson in life. Eventually, it would help to make him a wealthy man.

If ever there was an entrepreneur who understood the secret of successful business, it was Carnegie. He knew the implications of the little things. If you take care of them, the big things take care of themselves.

For those who operate a home business or are self-employed, a good application of this lesson is that seemingly small deductions and credits on your tax return can add up quickly. The trick is to find them and to know how to use them.

There are many ways for small business owners to take advantage of the tax laws that favor them. A wide array of deductions and tax-saving opportunities help entrepreneurs become "penny-wise and pound-smart." The best way to start saving is to learn more about taxes and being self-employed.

Self-Employment Tax

Some people believe that self-employment embodies the American dream. The joy of being your own boss, of answering to nobody, recalls simpler times of pioneers settling the West and fishermen casting their nets on the open sea.

But back then, cowpokes and seafaring types didn't have to deal with the small library that is our tax code, and they didn't have to worry about all the paperwork that today's entrepreneurs face.

As a self-employed individual, you'll start with the same tax form that we've been discussing—Form 1040. In addition to Form 1040, you'll also file Schedule C (or Schedule F if you're a farmer), on which you'll compute the net profit or loss from your business. A net profit is taxable income, and a net loss is usually deductible from other income. You'll also file Schedule SE, on which you'll compute your self-employment tax, which is not to be confused with the income tax.

Simply stated, **self-employment tax** is the basic equivalent of FICA (Federal Insurance Contribution Act), otherwise known as Social Security tax. For all people who operate their own businesses, big or small, this tax earmarks a portion of income for Social Security and Medicare. But self-employed individuals also receive a separate tax benefit. Unlike employed wage earners, self-employed people are allowed to deduct a portion of their Social Security and Medicare taxes on their Form 1040.

plain talk

Self-employment tax is an income tax levied on self-employed taxpayers. It consists of two parts—a Social Security tax and a Medicare tax.

Hobby or Business?

How do you know if an activity you engage in is a **hobby** or a business? The difference is important because hobby expenses are deductible only to the extent of the income you derive from the hobby, and then only as a limited itemized deduction.

Say, for example, that you take pictures as a hobby. Last year, a magazine purchased one of your pictures for $50. Because photography is a hobby for you, you must declare the $50 as taxable income. If you itemize deductions, you may claim up to $50 of your hobby expenses as a miscellaneous deduction.

However, if your activity is a business and your expenses exceed your business income, you may generally deduct your loss from your other income you may have. If, for example, your photography business is profit-motivated and it loses $3,000 for the year, you may usually reduce your taxable income from other sources by that amount.

As a general rule, the IRS will consider an activity to be a business with a profit motive if it is profitable in three of five consecutive years (some exceptions apply). However, this is merely a rule of thumb and can be refuted by either the IRS or the taxpayer. Traditionally, the IRS and the courts have used the following factors to determine if an activity is a business or a hobby:

- **Amount of occasional profits, if any, that are earned**
- **Degree of personal pleasure or recreation involved**
- **Expectation that the assets used in your business may appreciate in value**
- **Expertise of you and your advisors**
- **Financial status**
- **History of income and losses with respect to the activity**

- **Manner in which you carry on the activity**
- **Success in carrying on similar or dissimilar activities**
- **Time and effort you expend in carrying out this activity**

Making Estimated Tax Payments

A s we've mentioned, income taxes are a pay-as-you-go proposition. Taxes are due as the income is received. If you're employed, your employer usually helps you meet this obligation through payroll tax withholding. But if you're self-employed (or have a large amount of other income that is not subject to withholding), you're required to make quarterly tax payments to the United States Treasury. Such payments are called estimated payments.

Say, for example, that your only income is from your self-employment, and that you expect to have a $10,000 tax liability (a combination of income tax and self-employment tax, both reported on Form 1040) for the year. Assuming your income is fairly steady, you should make four quarterly estimated payments of about $2,500 each. Why not keep the money in the bank and pay the whole $10,000 on April 15? Because if you do, you'll get smacked with a penalty that will probably more than wipe out any interest the money may have earned.

There are different methods for determining how much quarterly tax to pay and how much to leave unpaid until you file your return. One method lets you pay the minimum required to avoid the penalty while another allows you to make quarterly payments so you will receive a refund, if that's what you want.

If you pay your taxes on a quarterly basis, you'll have to meet IRS calendar deadlines. Typically, that means payments are due April 15, June 15, September 15, and January 15 of the following calendar year. To pay estimated tax, send a check or money order with Form 1040-ES, after completing the worksheet that

THE CHALLENGE

Sara had a problem. The twenty-nine year old instructor started an equestrian program on her family's small ranch. When her business showed a loss because of start-up expenses and a slow economy, Sara deducted her loss from her other income. "No way," said the IRS, which declared her business a hobby, so Sara could deduct her expenses only to the extent of her lesson program income.

"When I read that letter, I knew right away that my tax bill would increase substantially if I couldn't prove my activity was a business," recalled Sara.

THE PLAN

A visit with Sara's tax professional revealed that she would need to provide evidence that she had a profit motive, even though revenues weren't yet substantial. When the IRS sees small businesses that don't make profits on a regular basis, the agency tends to view such businesses as hobbies.

In the portion of the regulations dealing with businesses and profits, there are few hard and fast rules to determine if a profit motive is present in a business. A business could lose money and still be considered a for-profit activity. It is important that all the facts and circumstances support a profit motive.

With that information in hand, Sara gathered evidence to support her claim of a profit motive, including newsletter and Web site advertisements, invoices for the lesson horse she purchased, a log of all the lessons she conducted by date and time, and copies of the checks Sara received from customers for instructing them.

"A few months later I heard back from the IRS that I was in the clear," Sara said. "It was important to me that the IRS thought I was running a legitimate business, not just running a fun horse program. The tax deductions are nice, but the acknowledgment of the hard work I'd put into my business was even better."

comes with it to determine the amount you should pay. Estimating the correct amount to pay can be tricky, and an error could expose you to a penalty. Our advice: Ask your tax professional to help you determine what your quarterly payments should be so you can achieve the goal you have in mind.

Setting Up Your Business in a Tax-Friendly Manner

When you decide to take the plunge and start your own business, you'll want to set your business up in the most tax-advantageous manner possible. Deciding what legal form your business will take is one of the most important start-up decisions you'll make. There are advantages and disadvantages to each form to consider, so it's a good idea to seek professional tax, financial, and legal advice before deciding.

Before we discuss the various legal forms your business can take, you'll need to know a little bit about passive activities. Passive activities are business activities in which you do not materially participate, and rental activities. Material participation means you are involved in the operation of the business on a regular, continuous, and substantial basis. Losses from passive activities generally can be deducted only to the extent you have income from other passive activities. (There is an exception for rental activities—see Chapter 6.) This rule applies to sole proprietorships, partners, and S corporation shareholders.

Sole Proprietorship—This means just what the words imply—you and you alone own the business. You're responsible for everything from the decision-making to all debts associated with the business. Generally speaking, the legal and record-keeping requirements are simpler for a sole proprietorship than for other forms of business, and no separate tax return is required. All necessary forms are included with your individual return.

fast fact

Only half of the self-employment tax is deductible. For 2002, the first $84,900 of your annual employment and self-employment income is subject to the Social Security tax, but there is no such limit for the Medicare tax.

smart step

If you are self-employed and you also hold a job, ask your employer to increase the income tax taken out of your paycheck by completing a new Form W-4. You may be able to avoid making quarterly tax payments.

As we said before, you are personally responsible for all business debts. But on the bright side, you can pay your spouse and children (under age twenty-one) reasonable wages for services performed and deduct them as an expense. In addition, you don't have to pay FUTA (unemployment tax) on their wages, or Social Security and Medicare taxes on your children's (under eighteen) wages. If your spouse works for you, you can also set up a plan to have the business pay for your family's medical insurance.

Partnership—In this type of business, you and at least one other person will run the show and take all the risks. A partnership files its own return, but does not pay income tax. All the income, deductions, gains, losses, and credits are passed through to the partners, who will include these items on their individual returns, even if they receive no money. A risk in this arrangement is that each general partner is responsible for all partnership debts to the extent of both the partnership's and their own personal assets.

A benefit of a partnership is that a married couple can be considered equal owners, which allows each spouse to obtain his or her own Social Security and Medicare coverage through self-employment tax. Children can also be made partners, which also may result in some income being taxed at a lower rate.

Taxable Corporations—Unlike a sole proprietorship in which you are solely responsible for all income and debts, taxable corporations are legally recognized entities encompassing all your business's revenues, assets, expenses, and liabilities. When a business owner starts a company with a large number of employees and intends to issue stock or raise capital, the option of corporation status is desirable because of its limited liability advantages. The main advantage is that the shareholders are not liable if something major goes awry. Only the company's assets are at risk. The worst loss you could suffer would be your investment and any debt guarantees that you may have made personally. Another advantage of the taxable corporation is that it can provide more tax-free fringe benefits than other forms of business. As with sole proprietorships, the spouse and children can be paid reasonable wages for services performed, but unlike a sole proprietorship, these wages are subject to FUTA, Social Security and Medicare tax—regardless of their ages, and these wages and their associated employment taxes (the employer's share of Social Security, Medicare, and unemployment taxes) can be deducted.

Some cautions about the taxable corporation route: the legal and record-keeping requirements are more complicated than for sole proprietorships. For instance, corporations must hold annual meetings and director meetings, and they are required to keep minutes and records of all directors' major decisions. Corporations file their taxes using a separate corporate tax return and generally a more complex bookkeeping system is needed to record business transactions. Finally, deciding to stop doing business is not a simple decision. The corporation must be liquidated and its remaining assets distributed, which is another event with tax consequences.

S Corporations—An S corporation has some of the characteristics of a corporation and some of the characteristics of a partnership. As with a partnership, an S corporation usually pays no tax; income, deductions, gains, losses, and credits are passed through to the shareholders who include them on their individual returns, even if they receive no money. As with a corporation, the shareholders have limited liability.

Not all corporations are eligible to be S corporations. Some of the requirements are: seventy-five or fewer shareholders; no more than one class of stock; and no nonresident alien shareholders. A corporation that wants to be an S corporation must file Form 2553.

fast fact

An individual's business activity may be operated as a sole proprietorship, partnership, limited liability company (LLC), taxable corporation, or S corporation.

Get competant
legal advice
when deciding
what form your
business should
take. It is one
of the most
important
decisions you'll
have to make.

Limited Liability Companies (LLC)—An LLC may be operated as a sole proprietorship, partnership, or corporation. A one-person LLC that is not incorporated is treated as a sole proprietorship. A multi-person LLC that is not incorporated is treated as a partnership unless it elects to be treated as incorporated. An LLC that is incorporated is treated as a taxable or S corporation.

A word of caution about the LLC: It is a relatively new type of business entity. Thus, there are many uncertainties about the tax and financial effects of its operations. Consult with your tax, financial, and legal advisors if you are considering an LLC.

Do I Get Any Special Breaks?

Most ordinary and necessary expenses of conducting your business are deductible, and it pays to take advantage of every legal deduction. Each deduction reduces not only your income tax, but your self-employment tax as well if your business takes the form of a sole proprietorship or partnership. You should familiarize yourself with all the deductions you may be eligible to claim, because there are a lot of deductions available. Use the following checklist to find key deductions for the self-employed.

Self-Employed Deductions Checklist

- [ ] **Advertising and promotional expenses**
- [ ] **Car and truck expenses**
- [ ] **Cost of products that you resell or cost of materials if you manufacture things for customers.** (Also include associated expenses such as freight charges)
- [ ] **Depreciation of various items, including vehicles, office equipment** (e.g., chairs, desks, lamps)**, cellular phones, and computer hardware**
- [ ] **Fees associated with professional organizations, such as the Chamber of Commerce, a trade union, or business association**
- [ ] **Half of your self-employment tax**
- [ ] **Health insurance premiums for employees**
- [ ] **Home-office expenses** (if you have a qualified home office)
- [ ] **Insurance**
- [ ] **Meals and entertainment expenses** (generally 50 percent deductible)
- [ ] **Mortgage interest or business property**
- [ ] **Office lease or rental payments, and any repairs or maintenance expenses**
- [ ] **Office supplies and postage**
- [ ] **Professional fees for lawyers, financial advisors, Web site designers, or anyone who assists you in the conduct of your business**
- [ ] **Start-up costs** (must be amortized over at least five years)
- [ ] **Subscriptions to business-related magazines, newsletters, and fee-based Web sites**
- [ ] **Taxes and licenses**
- [ ] **Tax preparation fees for business-related forms and schedules**
- [ ] **Travel expenses**
- [ ] **Utilities**
- [ ] **Wages to employees, if you have any**

With these deductions in mind, let's dig deeper into some tax-planning strategies you might want to consider as a self-employed business owner.

Depreciation

When you purchase business property that can be expected to last more than one year, it must be depreciated over its recovery period (the life assigned to the property under the tax law). Common recovery periods for property that is not real estate are three, five, and seven years. Residential rental property is depreciated over twenty-seven and a half years and nonresidential real property is depreciated over thirty-nine years.

Expensing—Expensing is a powerful tax strategy for business owners. Instead of depreciating property, you may be able to expense some of it (that is, write off the cost in the year you buy it). The most you can write off for 2002 is $24,000 ($25,000 for years after 2002). Real estate is not eligible. Property eligible for the expense deduction (the section 179 deduction, named for the section of the tax code that allows it) generally must be acquired by purchase.

The section 179 deduction cannot exceed your business income for the year. For this purpose, you can include wages and salaries and, if you are married and filing a joint return, your spouse's business income and wages and salaries. So, if you are operating at a loss, you cannot increase your loss by claiming the section 179 deduction. Other restrictions apply as well.

New 30 Percent Bonus Depreciation—Under a provision enacted in 2002, you are allowed to deduct 30 percent of the basis of the property placed in service in 2002 in addition to the usual depreciation. Real property is not eligible for this deduction. If you do not want to take the additional 30 percent deduction, you must say so in a statement attached to your return.

The depreciation deduction for most vehicles you acquired in 2002 for use in your business is generally limited to $3,060. But, if you claim the 30 percent allowance, the limit is $7,660. If you also use the vehicle for non-business purposes, the above limits are multiplied by the business-use percentage. Note, however, that vehicles with a gross weight of more than 6,000 pounds are not subject to the $3,060 or $7,660 limit. In applying the 6,000 pound test, use the unloaded weight for automobiles and the gross vehicle weight, *not* the unloaded weight, for trucks and vans.

Choosing a Depreciation Method—Here are some items to consider before choosing your depreciation method. If you expect to be in a higher tax bracket in future years, consider foregoing both the section 179 deduction and the 30 percent allowance. Also consider using slower depreciation methods. If you have an immediate need for cash, claim the largest allowable depreciation deduction. You can reduce your overall self-employment tax by claiming the largest depreciation deduction. When you sell the property, gain attributable to depreciation is not subject to self-employment tax. Be aware that this may reduce the Social Security benefits you receive when you retire.

Eat, Drink, and Be Tax Happy

A valuable deduction is the tax law's meals and entertainment allowance. You can generally deduct half of these expenses, provided they relate specifically to your business. Use a log to keep track of the date, time, amount paid, attendees, and business purpose of the meal or entertainment, or write all this on the receipt itself. You'll only need the receipt if the expenditure was $75 or more. These expenses can add up pretty quickly and take a nice chunk out of your tax burden.

For every gift you give to a business client, you can also deduct up to $25 (or the cost of the gift, if less), but you are limited to one gift per client per year. Promotional gifts that cost $4 or less each on which your name is clearly and permanently imprinted are deductible as an advertising expense and aren't included in the $25 limit.

smart step

Be savvy about the way you manage your business's money at year-end. Billing late can push income into the following tax year, and buying before the new year can add deductions to this tax year.

Deferring Income

The strategy to defer income is simple: If you are a cash-basis taxpayer, do not include in current-year income any amount received after midnight on December 31. That income is included in your income for the following year. Even if deferring income to the next year doesn't change your marginal tax rate, you still win by delaying the tax on that income until next year.

Deferring income generally applies only to the self-employed and not to traditional employee wage earners. Under the law, income is taxable in the year it is constructively received. That means if you have possession of it, you include it in income on the day you receive it. For example, if you receive a check on December 31, you must include it in income, even if you cannot cash or deposit the check until January 2.

If you want to increase your current-year deductions, consider accelerating your expenses. If you're a cash-basis taxpayer, you can normally deduct only expenditures that are paid in the current year. For example, if you know you will need certain supplies in January, buy and pay for them in December. But you generally cannot deduct expenses paid in advance. Examples include interest on a loan and insurance payments. For example, if you pay $1,200 in June for a one-year insurance policy, you can deduct $700 in the current year and $500 in the following year.

Deferring income or accelerating expenses may be a good tax strategy, but remember, the goals and needs of your business should always come first and must be weighed carefully before making any last-minute tax-planning moves.

Hiring Your Children

Sole proprietors often need all the help they can get, and many hire their children to work in their businesses. Hiring your children can also be a worthwhile tax-saving strategy. In order to implement it, you must pay reasonable wages for the work actually performed by your children. You'll receive a deduction for the wages paid. If the children are under eighteen years of age, there are no Social Security or federal unemployment taxes, and they can shelter up to $4,700 (for 2002) of wage income with their available standard deduction.

To deduct wages paid to your children, the amount you pay must be reasonable for the work performed.

How much savings can you get from this strategy? Let's assume your marginal tax rate is 27 percent and you pay 15.3 percent self-employment tax. Have one of your children pitch in during the summer and pay him or her $7.50 per hour. Have him or her work 320 hours (about two months out of the summer vacation). Your gross cost: $2,400. Your tax savings: about $941. Your net cost: about $1,459. The experience: priceless. Well, maybe. At any rate, this is a useful tax strategy, and everybody in the family wins. That is, if you're a fair boss and your kids are helpful workers.

If you incorporated your business, you won't receive quite the same children-friendly tax treatment if you hire your kids. The deduction for wages is taken on the corporation's tax return and the children's wages are subject to Social Security and federal unemployment taxes regardless of age. Still, it could be a great way to help your child earn some money, gain some valuable experience, keep some of your money in the family, and provide you with the help you need.

Traveling

Self-employed taxpayers can claim a number of travel-related deductions.

Automobile Expenses—Automobiles are expensive for businesses to own and operate. It helps that the IRS lets business owners defray some of these costs by deducting business-related vehicle expenses. For 2002, you can deduct 36.5 cents per business mile or the business percentage of your actual costs, whichever is larger. In either case, you may also deduct business-related parking fees and tolls. Be sure to keep track of all business miles and expenses in a log, which you can keep handy in your glove compartment.

Flying the Tax-Friendly Skies—Where does the IRS draw the line between business travel and recreational travel? If you're self-employed, you'll find it's currently drawn in your favor. Wherever the trip was taken, if you can prove it is directly related to your business, you can deduct it. Before you say, "Kansas City, here we come," make sure your business reasons are legitimate.

Deductible expenses include the cost of hotel accommodations, 50 percent of meals and business-related entertainment, round-trip travel expenses, and seminar or convention fees. This is another deduction that can make a big difference. If the traveling entrepreneur also participates in some non-business activities while on the trip, the travel expenses may need to be prorated between business and non-business activities. The cost of non-business expenses at the business location is not deductible.

Don't go crazy with excitement; there are some limits here. The expenses can't be lavish or extravagant and must be business related. If your business is selling power tools and you decide to attend an underwater basket weaving convention in Fiji, the cost of the trip is not going to be deductible.

Home-Office Deductions

As the demand on people's available time continues to climb, many people, whether employed or self-employed, occasionally use a portion of their home for work purposes. The question is whether or not that work use results in tax-deductible home-office expenses. In order to qualify, there are certain requirements that must be met. If you qualify, the expenses of operating your home office are deductible.

Is My Home Office Deductible?

The following guidelines related to the flowchart on the following page can determine if your home office expenses are deductible.

Exclusively for business use—Your home office must be used exclusively for business. The standard is strict and means that you cannot make personal use of the office at any time. Your home office can be an entire room or only part of a room. There are some exceptions for portions of your home used for day care or inventory storage.

Used regularly for business—In order to deduct your home office expenses, you must spend a substantial amount of time in your home office on a regular basis.

CAN YOU DEDUCT HOME-OFFICE* EXPENSES?

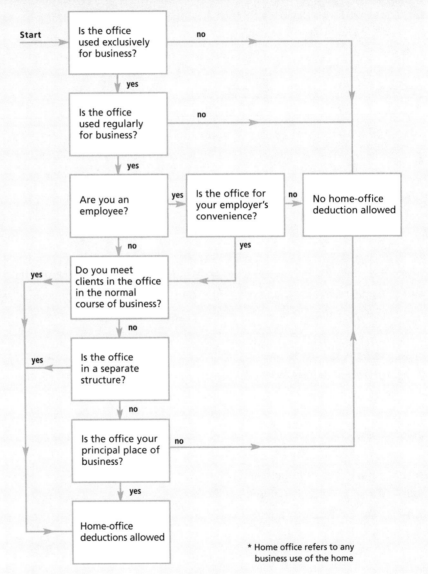

Start → Is the office used exclusively for business? — no →

yes ↓

Is the office used regularly for business? — no →

yes ↓

Are you an employee? — yes → Is the office for your employer's convenience? — no → No home-office deduction allowed

no ↓ (Are you an employee?)

yes ↓ (Is the office for your employer's convenience?)

Do you meet clients in the office in the normal course of business? — yes →

no ↓

Is the office in a separate structure? — yes →

no ↓

Is the office your principal place of business? — no →

yes ↓

Home-office deductions allowed

* Home office refers to any business use of the home

Source: H&R Block

Use by employees—If you are an employee you cannot deduct your home-office expenses unless your employer requires the office. If you simply take work home, your office won't qualify. The office must be for the employer's convenience, not yours.

Office used to meet clients—If you meet clients, patients, or customers in your home office during the normal course of business, the office may qualify even if it isn't your principal place of business.

Separate structure—If your home office is located on your property, but it is not physically attached to your residence, your home office may still qualify for the deduction even if it isn't your principal place of business.

Principal place of business—Unless you meet clients in your office, or it's a separate structure, your home office must be your principal place of business. It meets this standard if you perform administrative functions there, such as billing and contacting clients, provided you have no other fixed location where you perform such tasks.

Did You Qualify?

Once you've established that you qualify for a home-office deduction, you will need to identify deductible expenses and keep good records to enable your return to be prepared and filed. Form 8829, Expenses for Business Use of Your Home, is used to record these deductions for sole proprietors.

To be eligible
for a home-
office deduc-
tion, you must
generally use
your home of-
fice exclusively
and regularly
for business.
Other require-
ments apply
as well.

If you own your home, you may deduct the business portion of your mortgage interest and real estate taxes. If you rent, you may deduct the business portion of that expense. In either case, you may deduct the business portion of utilities and insurance.

Expenses incurred solely for business purposes need not be prorated. Examples include repairs to the office, insurance on business equipment and liability coverage for the business, the cost of a telephone line exclusively for your business, and long-distance business calls and wireless phone expenses for your business.

Your deduction for business use of your home cannot exceed the income for your business computed without regard to this deduction. Any excess is carried forward to the next year. In addition, the expenses must be deducted in a specific order. See IRS Publication 587 for more details.

Get Organized

Are you having problems getting your business records organized? Check out the tax record-keeping tips below and you'll be feeling better in no time:

- **Keep business and personal tax records separate.** This includes separate bank accounts and credit cards.
- **Make a filing system for all records and receipts to support income and expenses claimed.**
- **Use your travel log every time you use your vehicle for business, and keep it in your glove box for easy access.**
- **Reconcile your bank and credit card statements each month.**
- **Highlight all long-distance business calls on your home phone bill and keep them in your business records.**
- **Get in the habit of asking for a receipt for every business expense and save them all.**

- **Use a credit card or check to pay all business expenses.** This will automatically provide written evidence of the expense.
- **Keep all records and receipts in a safe, dry location for future use.** Consider a safe deposit box for crucial records.

Being self-employed can be both a rewarding and challenging experience. Part of the challenge is to make sure that you learn about and take advantage of the many tax-saving opportunities that exist for the self-employed. Reducing your tax liability should be rewarding.

the ESSENTIALS

1

Self-employment tax is a tax for self-employed people regardless of the size of their business. The self-employment tax includes both Social Security and Medicare taxes.

2

Self-employed people can deduct half their self-employment tax in computing their adjusted gross income.

3

Self-employed individuals generally pay their taxes on an estimated basis. There are various methods for determining how much quarterly tax to pay and how much to leave unpaid until you file your return. Ask your tax professional to help you determine what your quarterly payments should be so you can achieve the goal you have in mind.

4

From the IRS's perspective, you must have a profit motive for your activity to be considered a business.

5 Deciding whether to establish your business as a sole proprietorship, partnership, taxable corporation, S corporation, or limited liability company is one of the first and most important decisions when starting a business.

6 To deduct home-office expenses, you must generally use the office exclusively and regularly for business. Other requirements apply.

9 [BACK TO SCHOOL:

Using Your Tax Plan to
Fund Educational Expenses]

"The avoidance of taxes is the only intellectual pursuit
that carries any reward."
—John Maynard Keynes

smart step

Start saving for your child's college expenses as soon as possible. The earlier you start, the more help you'll get from compounded earnings.

Our nation values education, and we put our money where our mouth is. The government offers an abundance of tax benefits to help Americans save and pay for college. From education savings accounts you can start when your child is an infant, to tax credits available to children of all ages (even those in their second childhood), Uncle Sam goes out of his way to help you get an education. He does this in part via the tax code.

Where to Start

Back when the price of a four-year degree from State U wasn't the same as a small home (or, at some schools, a big one), saving for college meant putting away money in a savings account, investing in some conservative U.S. Treasury Bonds, or opening a custodial account.

But this strategy just doesn't cut it anymore, because the cost of a college education is rising about 5.8 percent annually for a four-year private school and 9.9 percent annually for a public school. These days, parents—and sometimes grandparents—are starting earlier and investing more wisely to get children through State U or Harvard. Part of college planning for your child or grandchild should involve learning about every tax break available. Make your money work for you in every way you possibly can.

The best time to start planning for college is, of course, as soon as possible after your child or grandchild is born. As with other investments, you need to start saving while time is still on your side. There are plenty of options to help you in the years leading up to college and beyond, and all of them have important tax implications. Check out some of these tax-savvy options:

- **529 Qualified Tuition Programs** (i.e. college savings accounts and prepaid tuition plans)

- **Coverdell education savings accounts** (also known as education savings accounts or ESAs)
- **Roth and traditional IRAs**
- **UTMA or UGMA accounts** (custodial accounts)
- **Student loan interest and tuition fees deductions**
- **Hope and lifetime learning credits**
- **Stocks**
- **Series EE or I U.S. Government savings bonds**

Let's take a look at each of them.

529 Qualified Tuition Programs (QTP)

A great place to start your child's college fund is through college savings plans, also known as 529 plans. Formerly only state-sponsored institutions could establish these plans, but now private educational institutions can also sponsor their own plans. Distributions from 529 state-sponsored plans for qualified expenses escape federal income tax and may be free of state income tax as well. In addition, some states offer a deduction for contributions.

The 529 plans come in two varieties: college savings plans and prepaid tuition plans.

College Savings Plans—For a minimal amount, anyone—parents, relatives, and even friends—can open a college savings plan and contribute regularly to build a tax-free college fund for a child. Your investment grows tax-free for as long as you remain invested in the plan. Plus, if your family's college plans change, you may change the beneficiary of the plan to another family member without federal income tax consequences.

Benefits of 529 Savings Plans

They're a terrific tax break—Earnings are tax-free, and withdrawals from state-sponsored plans for qualified educational expenses are exempt from federal income taxes.

They're easy to set up—Simply choose an investment option—a large cap fund, a balanced fund, or a bond fund, for example—and contribute to the fund regularly.

Many are deductible on your state tax return—Some states allow you to deduct your contributions on your state return. Because rules vary from state to state, be sure to check with your state tax office for details.

You will likely get professional help—Some of the best-known money managers in the United States offer 529 college savings plans. Once you sign up and begin contributing, your money manager will take care of the rest, including management and administration of the fund. As with any investment, check on the plan's past performance before you invest.

How the money is withdrawn is up to you—If your child decides not to go to college, you can transfer the fund to another beneficiary. If the money is not used for qualified educational expenses, the earnings are taxable and may be subject to a 10 percent penalty.

They're flexible—In most cases, 529 plans are open to state residents and nonresidents alike. Under the tax laws enacted in 2001, you can now roll your 529 plan over from one state to another with no tax consequence or penalty. This might be a big consideration if you expect to move during junior's childhood.

They're generous—Generally, you are allowed to invest more compared to other tax-favored education-related savings plans.

They're good for estate planning—Contributions to 529 plans are powerful estate planning options for grandparents, because the money is not included in the grandparent's taxable estate.

Most states do have limits, but many are generously high and some allow in excess of $200,000 to be saved tax-free. So what if you don't happen to live in one of those states? Don't worry, because many states will allow you to participate, regardless of where you live. But check carefully because some states require that the contributor or student be a resident.

Money invested in a 529 college savings plan isn't just for college tuition. You can also use plan money for room and board, fees, and other expenses. There are no age limits, so even older Americans with a desire to go back to school can participate.

There are some potential downsides to investing in a 529 college savings plan. If your plan has limited investment options, it may be a challenge to get the performance you want or need. With some plans, you can jump from one investment class to another only once a year. Also be aware that eligibility for financial aid may be affected by the account or distributions.

smart step

Investigate the past performance of a 529 plan before investing.

▶ What to Look for in a 529 College Savings Plan

- **A plan with many options**—Check for plans with a wide variety of investment options.
- **Reasonable fees**—Generally, fees should be in line with mutual funds that are similar.
- **Consistent performance**—Double-check the plan's past performance. A plan with lots of ups and downs is something to avoid.

Prepaid Tuition Plans—These plans are known for helping you lock in tomorrow's tuition costs at today's prices. In return for a lump sum, or a series of payments, the state guarantees to cover your child's tuition and fees at a state college or university. Generally speaking, your contributions will be invested by the plan to grow at a rate sufficient to match the anticipated inflation rate of tuition at these state schools. As with college savings accounts, you may change the beneficiary of the plan to another family member without federal income tax consequences if your child's college plans change.

THE CHALLENGE

Brian and Judy had devoted their lives to making sure that all their children received the best possible start in life. Everything in each of their children's lives was going along just fine. Then one day Brian realized that the education savings account he and his wife had been investing in for his oldest son Joseph's education wasn't going to meet their son's college expenses.

One day on the golf course, Brian heard from one of the members of his foursome about a 529 college savings plan that he had invested in for his son. Brian learned that the account could provide great tax breaks and offer many investment options. He decided that he needed to get more information as the clock was ticking toward the time when his son would really need the money.

THE PLAN

Brian called a financial advisor and scheduled an appointment. The advisor thoroughly explained the benefits of the 529 plan and confirmed that Brian could stay in control. "I'd heard a story about some other kind of account where the kid took the money and wasted it on buying cars and throwing parties for his friends," said Brian. "I don't think my son would do that, but I needed to be sure."

The financial advisor showed Brian investment options for 529 plans, and he explained how the funds could be shifted periodically to gain higher returns or minimize the risks to the account balance as his son got closer to college. Brian liked to have choices, but he didn't want to try picking individual stocks. He also liked that his son's grandparents could contribute to the plan. Brian and Judy contributed generous amounts to the account and the couple were soon back on track toward being able to fund their son's college education. The advisor assured Brian that should his son's college plans change, the account could be changed to benefit one of his other two sons, Robby or Peter.

Drawbacks to prepaid tuition plans include earning a rate of return that attempts only to match the projected rise in tuition costs for the state schools. So if your child gets accepted to Yale, you can use the money you invested in the State U prepaid college plan to send him to school in Connecticut, but it may not cover all the expenses. Also be aware that eligibility for financial aid may be affected by participation in the plan.

Coverdell Education Savings Accounts

The Coverdell education savings account is another college savings plan with strong tax benefits. These accounts are also called "ESAs." Once known as "education IRAs," ESAs are similar to 529 plans, except they give you somewhat more freedom in how you can allocate the money saved in the accounts. ESAs don't apply to college only: you can withdraw money tax-free to pay for qualified elementary, secondary, and higher education tuition, fees, and expenses. Beginning in 2002, you can invest in both a 529 plan and an ESA for the same beneficiary for the same year. Now Americans can use both to meet their education planning needs.

ESAs do have limits. Annual contributions are capped at $2,000 per beneficiary, and you don't receive a tax deduction for your contributions. The real value of the account is the tax-free status of funds when withdrawn for qualified educational expenses. If your modified adjusted gross income exceeds $190,000 ($95,000 on a single return), the allowable contribution will be reduced or eliminated. If you find yourself in this situation, you might want to have a grandparent handle the investment for you. You could give $2,000 to the grandparent who in turn could make the contribution for you (assuming he or she is eligible).

Contributions to ESAs must generally be made before the beneficiary turns eighteen years old, and the money must be distributed before age thirty. Any unused balance can be rolled over to another child's account. Because many financial institutions offer ESAs, it's relatively easy to switch accounts. In addition, you can claim a Hope credit or lifetime learning credit in the same year as you take a tax-free ESA withdrawal, but you can't use the same expenses claimed for the Hope or the lifetime learning credit and the ESA distribution.

Roth and Traditional IRAs

Both Roth and traditional IRAs have proven to be practical investment tools. Not only do they provide excellent retirement savings benefits, but both can be used for college savings, too. You can take distributions from your Roth or traditional IRA for qualified higher education expenses without paying the 10 percent penalty that is levied on early (under age fifty-nine and a half) distributions. While you won't have to pay the early distribution penalty, the amount of the distribution included in your income tax is computed in the usual manner. Also be aware that these accounts and distributions could affect the ability to get financial aid.

UTMA or UGMA Accounts

UTMA and UGMA are acronyms for the Uniform Transfers/Gifts to Minors Act. These custodial accounts are losing popularity as other education savings vehicles have been introduced. In the past, these accounts were very popular and played an important role in many families' college savings programs. One advantage to using a custodial account to save for college is its ability to reduce the family's tax bill. Until age fourteen, the first $750 of a child's investment earnings is tax-free, and the next $750 is taxed at the child's rate (usually 10 percent). After that, the parents' marginal rate applies.

There are some advantages to UTMA and UGMA accounts, but the benefits derived from other plans (529 plans and ESAs) significantly diminish the attractiveness of this approach to college savings. Another important point about custodial accounts is that your contributions to the account are considered an irrevocable gift. Once the student reaches the age of majority (usually eighteen or twenty-one), the account belongs to the student, and he or she can use the money for anything—like a shiny new Corvette for an all-expenses-paid road trip. Also be aware that ownership of a custodial account may cause the student to qualify for less financial aid.

If you've invested in a UTMA or UGMA account and want to invest the assets in a 529 plan, you must sell the securities, report any gains on the child's return, and put the cash into the 529 plan. Finally, another note of caution: Unlike a 529 plan, you won't be able to change the beneficiary of the custodial account and name another child as the beneficiary.

Student Loan Interest Deduction

If you obtained a loan to help pay for college expenses, you can deduct up to $2,500 annually of the interest you pay on the loan. You can take this write-off whether or not you itemize deductions. This deduction applies to interest on almost any loan (not just federal student loans) that you used exclusively for qualified higher education expenses for yourself, your spouse, and for a person who was your dependent at the time you borrowed the money. Your MAGI can affect the amount of your deduction.

Before 2002, the deduction for student loan interest was available only for the first sixty months that interest payments were due. For 2002 and later years, the sixty-month limit no longer applies. If you stopped taking this deduction because your sixty-month time limit expired, start taking it again.

smart step

Education costs to upgrade your job skills may be deductible if you itemize deductions. Be sure to compare the benefit from this deduction with those available from the lifetime learning credit and the tuition and fees deduction to determine your best option.

Tuition and Fees Deduction

For 2002, you may also be able to deduct up to $3,000 you paid for higher education tuition and fees for yourself, your spouse, and your dependent. Like the student loan interest deduction, this deduction can be taken whether or not you itemize deductions. It may be limited by certain nontaxable assistance you may have received for your qualified expenses, such as scholarships and grants. Your MAGI can affect the amount of your deduction.

The Hope Credit

The Hope credit allows you a tax credit of up to $1,500 for each qualifying student who meets the following four qualifications. The student must:

1. Be in his or her first two years of post-secondary education
2. Be enrolled in a program that leads to a degree or other recognized educational credential
3. Be enrolled at least half time for at least one academic period during the year
4. Have no history of a felony drug conviction

Under the Hope credit, you can claim 100 percent of the first $1,000 and 50 percent of the next $1,000 of qualified expenses, which include tuition, fees, and books that must be purchased from the educational institution. This is a per-child credit, meaning you'll receive a tax credit of up to $1,500 for every qualifying student.

As with the other tax credits, your MAGI affects your benefits. For single taxpayers, the 2002 Hope credit begins phasing out when your MAGI exceeds $41,000 and completely disappears at $51,000. For those who are married and file jointly, the MAGI phase-out range is between $82,000 and $102,000. Individuals who use the married and filing separately status are not eligible to claim the credit.

The Lifetime Learning Credit

R equirements for claiming the lifetime learning credit are less restrictive than for the Hope credit, but the lifetime learning credit provides less generous benefits. This credit is available for expenses relating to all years of post-secondary education including graduate-level courses. In addition, there is no pursuit-of-a-degree or at-least-half-time enrollment requirement, and the felony drug conviction rule does not apply.

The credit is equal to 20 percent of the first $5,000 you pay for qualified expenses for all eligible students in your family. Thus, the maximum credit you can claim for your family is limited to $1,000 annually. For 2003, the $5,000/$1,000 amounts are $10,000 and $2,000, respectively.

Your MAGI can affect the amount of your credit in the same manner as the Hope credit, mentioned earlier.

――――――――――――――――――― **Tax Benefits for Higher Education**
The following chart discusses some of the differences among the various options for funding college expenses. Generally, you may not claim more than one benefit for the same education expense. Check with your tax professional to determine which option is best for you.

smart step

If you take the Hope or lifetime learning credit for a student, you cannot take the tuition and fees deduction for that student. Consult your tax professional to determine which tax break saves you more.

COMPARISON OF TAX BENEFITS FOR EDUCATION

	Savings Bond Interest Exclusion	529 Qualified Tuition Programs	Coverdell ESA*	Traditional and Roth IRAs*	Student Loan Interest Deduction	Tuition and Fees Deduction	Lifetime Learning Credit	Hope Credit
What is the benefit?	Interest is not taxed	Earnings are not taxed		No 10% additional tax on early distributions	Deduct the interest even if you don't itemize	Deduct expenses even if you don't itemize	Credits reduce your tax dollar-for-dollar	
What is the annual limit?	Amount of interest used for qualifying expenses	None	$2,000 contribution per beneficiary	Amount of qualifying expenses	$2,500	Up to $3,000 per family	Up to $1,000 per family	Up to $1,500 per student
What education applies?	All undergraduate and graduate study		Elementary, secondary, undergraduate, and graduate study	All undergraduate and graduate study				1st and 2nd years of undergraduate study
Are benefits limited by income?	Yes	No	Yes	No	Yes	Yes	Yes	Yes
What are some of the other conditions that apply?**	Applies only to qualified series EE bonds issued after 1989 and series I bonds	Distributions of earnings not used for qualified higher education expenses are subject to an additional 10% tax	Most beneficiaries must use up accounts or transfer them to a qualified relative before age 30	Taxable income from the distribution is computed using the usual rules	Loan proceeds must have been used exclusively for qualified educational expenses	Cannot claim both this deduction and a tax credit for education expenses for the same student in one year

Qualified expenses must be reduced by a tax-free distribution from a Coverdell ESA, QTP, and by excluded interest from savings bonds used for education | | Can be claimed only for 2 years

Must be enrolled at least half-time in a degree program

No history of a felony drug conviction |

* Any nontaxable withdrawal is limited to the amount that does not exceed qualifying educational expenses.
** Other conditions may apply. Please consult your tax professional or IRS Publication 970 for more details.

Source: H&R Block

Gifting Stocks

You may want to give your college student stocks or other securities that have appreciated. This strategy could serve to reduce your tax bill and help you to pay for his or her tuition at the same time. How is this possible? Well, the gain (and the associated tax bill) on the appreciated value of the stock will be passed along to the recipient of your gift. Most likely, your child's marginal tax rate is lower than yours, so the tax bill will be smaller.

How does it work? Let's say that several years ago you invested $5,000 in stock that is now worth $10,000. You also find yourself needing to pay your child's tuition expenses and decide to sell the stock to do so. If you sell the stock yourself, you will owe about $1,000 tax on the $5,000 gain (assuming the 20 percent long-term capital gains rate applies), leaving you a net of $9,000 to pay for the tuition. On the other hand, if you give your child the stock and then he or she sells it, the tax due would only be $400 (assuming he or she falls into the 10 or 15 percent bracket and the 8 percent long-term capital gains rate applies), resulting in a $500 savings. By giving your child the stock to sell, you are able to capitalize on his or her lower tax bracket.

One word of caution: This strategy could cost you a dependency exemption if the value of the gift means that your child contributes more than 50 percent of his or her support. See Chapter 3 for more information on the requirements for claiming a dependency exemption.

fast fact

The Hope and lifetime learning credits are nonrefundable. Any credit remaining after your tax liability has been reduced to zero will not be refunded to you.

What about the "Kiddie Tax?"

As we mentioned earlier in the chapter, it is a good idea to start saving for college as soon as possible, accumulating all the earnings on your investments you can in the process. Another consideration is the so-called **"kiddie tax."** This tax was enacted to prevent parents from reducing their tax by shifting their investment earnings to their children. With the kiddie tax, the first $750 of your child's unearned income is tax-free, the next $750 is taxed at the 10 percent rate, and the balance of the income is taxed at the parents' rate. The child must be under fourteen for the kiddie tax to apply; otherwise, the child's income will be taxed at his or her regular rates.

Assuming your child's only income is the $1,500 unearned income maximum, the tax due would only be $75. The first $750 income is received tax-free and the next $750 is taxed at the 10 percent rate. Compare this to your marginal rate. If you fall into the 27 percent bracket, the tax on $1,500 is $405. By shifting the income to your child, you save $330.

Buying U.S. savings bonds is a good option because recognition of the income can be deferred until the bond is actually cashed. If the child cashes the bonds after he or she turns fourteen, the interest that accumulated until then will be taxed at the child's rate. Tax-savvy parents may opt to purchase the bonds in their own names instead of the child's. If a parent owns the bonds and then cashes them in specifically to pay for the child's college expenses, the earnings can often be received tax-free.

Another way to leverage the kiddie tax is via stocks or other securities that have good potential for growth. This is often accomplished by establishing a custodial account. Tax on the stock's appreciation in value is deferred until the stock is sold. If the stock or security pays dividends or has capital gain distributions,

plain talk

The "kiddie tax" is not a specific tax on income, but rather a limitation on how much unearned income ($1,500) a child under fourteen can have before the parents' marginal rate is applied.

the income will be taxed at the child's rate unless the child's unearned income exceeds $1,500.

Keep in mind that the child must actually own the assets for this strategy to work. When the child reaches the age of majority, you lose control of the money. Also, by owning the assets, your child's ability to obtain financial aid may be affected because these assets will be factored in when determining a student's financial need.

Great Benefits from the 2001 Tax Bill

The 2001 tax bill provided numerous education benefits to taxpayers. Here's a snapshot of the benefits derived from the tax law:

The 2001 Tax Bill:

- **Eliminated taxes on distributions from state prepaid-tuition programs and college-savings plans.** Private institutions can now set up prepaid tuition plans. Income earned in these plans is not currently taxable. Distributions used for qualified higher education expenses are tax-free beginning in 2004.
- **Eliminated the sixty-month limit on deducting student-loan interest payments.** It also increased the MAGI for claiming the deduction. The phase-out range is now between $50,000 and $65,000. For married taxpayers filing jointly, it's between $100,000 and $130,000 MAGI.
- **Increased the annual limit on contributions to Coverdell ESAs, formerly known as education IRAs, from $500 to $2,000.** It also allowed tax-free distributions from the accounts to pay for qualified elementary and secondary education in addition to higher education expenses.

**smart
step**

If you cash in qualified U.S. savings bonds and use them for qualified education expenses, you may be able to exclude savings bond interest from income. Income limits apply.

■ Made permanent the exclusion for employer-provided tuition assistance, and even expanded it to cover graduate and professional courses.

■ Introduced a new above-the-line deduction for qualified higher education tuition and related expenses. If you are a single taxpayer whose MAGI is $65,000 or less ($130,000 or less for married couples filing jointly), you can deduct up to $3,000 per year in college tuition in 2002 and 2003, and up to $4,000 per year in 2004 and 2005. For 2004 and 2005, you can deduct up to $2,000 if your MAGI exceeds the $65,000/$130,000 limits, but does not exceed $80,000 ($160,000 for married couples filing jointly). If your MAGI exceeds the $80,000 or $160,000 limit, no deduction is allowed. This short-term provision expires after 2005. Before you take advantage of this deduction, check with your tax professional to make sure this is a better option for you than the Hope credit or the lifetime learning credit.

Keep in mind that these changes are from a single piece of legislation. New tax laws are enacted almost every year, and that's not all. The IRS issues new regulations and procedures regularly, and the courts make rulings that affect many of us. It's just plain smart to keep up with the changing tax picture.

the ESSENTIALS

1

Get an early start on saving for your child's college education. College costs continue to rise annually, so parents can use all the tax breaks they can get. Fortunately, there are several to choose from.

2

State-sponsored college savings plans and prepaid tuition plans, also known as 529 plans, are great tax savers. Distributions from state-sponsored 529 plans for qualified expenses are free from federal income tax and often state income tax as well. Some states allow a deduction for contributions to these plans.

3

Once known as education IRAs, Coverdell education savings accounts have many of the advantages of 529 plans, but they allow you a wider choice of investments. One disadvantage is the $2,000 limit on contributions for any beneficiary. You can withdraw money from an ESA tax-free to pay for qualified elementary, secondary, and higher education tuition, fees, and expenses.

4

The student loan interest deduction and tuition and fees deduction are available whether or not you itemize your deductions.

5

The Hope credit and lifetime learning credit will offset your tax liability dollar-for-dollar.

6

Planning for college expenses can be complicated. Contact your tax professional and financial advisor to determine what options are best for you.

10 [**READY-SET-GO: Preparing and Filing Your Tax Return**]

"Genius is one percent inspiration and ninety-nine percent perspiration."
—Thomas A. Edison

smart step

Start early gathering all the documents you'll need when you visit your tax professional or when you prepare your return yourself.

When it comes to saving money on a tax return, preparation is the key to opportunity.

To paraphrase the famous quote by Thomas Edison, filing your taxes without having a good strategy and records is 1 percent preparation and 99 percent perspiration. The smart tax planner has a different formula: 99 percent preparation and 1 percent execution.

That's not to downplay the execution part of the process. After all, if an electrician wires the room you added to your house, you still have to flip the switch to get the lights to work.

If you do a great job of preparing for it, completing your tax return is easy. Preparing—that's the hard part. That's why most of this book is about preparing a tax plan. The first nine chapters were designed to help you understand the tax code, help you learn about tax deductions, credits, and exemptions, and help you prepare a tax plan that covers your family, home, finances, business, and education. The goal of this chapter is to help you pull all that information together so you or your tax professional can prepare and file your return, helping you save as much on your taxes as the law allows.

Choose Your Own Tax Day

To most people, Tax Day means April 15, but don't wait until then. That is precisely the day you don't want to prepare and file your tax return. Why wait until the last minute when time is short and tensions are high, just to get caught in a stampede? Waiting will add to your stress level and could add to your tax liability if everything doesn't work out right. In Chapter 2 we discussed dividing tax planning into seasons. Well, April comes in the spring, but we recommend that you start your spring cleaning activities a little early. As soon as you have all your necessary tax-related information, pick any day you like and make it your own personal tax day. The earlier your return is prepared and filed, the sooner you'll get your refund, and the less likely you'll be to overlook tax benefits to which you're entitled.

Once you've picked your personal tax day, you'll need to decide who is going to prepare and file your return. As we said early on, we think using a tax professional is highly advisable. Not only will that person be able to assist you with tax planning throughout the year, but he or she can also prepare and file your return when the time comes. If you prepare and file your return yourself, there are software and online options to consider, and we'll discuss those in Chapter 12. In the rest of this chapter, we'll talk about things you'll need to consider regardless of who prepares and files your return.

One to Get Ready . . .

First make a list. Write down all the things you think you'll need when you see your tax professional or prepare your own return. The more complete your list, the less likely it is that you'll forget something and end up having to make another trip or two between your home and the tax professional's office. The list will also help you think through all the questions you will need to have answered or the things you want to point out to your tax professional. You've taken the time to buy and read this book, so make it work for you.

Tax Preparation Checklist

Your tax preparation checklist should look something like this:

✓ ───► **Personal Data**

- [ ] Information on how much alimony you paid to an ex-spouse and his/her Social Security number
- [ ] Names, addresses, and tax I.D.s or Social Security numbers for child-care providers and domestic employees
- [ ] Social Security numbers for all family members and dependents
- [ ] Tax returns for the previous two years

✓ ──────────► **Employment and Non-Investment Income Data**

- [ ] Alimony received
- [ ] Capital gains and losses
- [ ] Gambling and lottery winnings: Form W-2G (if applicable)
- [ ] Jury duty pay
- [ ] Miscellaneous income: Form 1099-MISC
- [ ] Partnership, S corporation, estate, and trust income: Schedules K-1
- [ ] Pensions and annuities: Forms 1099-R
- [ ] Prizes and awards
- [ ] Rental income and expenses
- [ ] Scholarships and fellowships
- [ ] Social Security and Railroad Retirement benefits: Forms SSA-1099, RRB-1099, and RRB-1099-R
- [ ] State and local income tax refunds: Form 1099-G
- [ ] Tip income
- [ ] Unemployment compensation: Form 1099-G
- [ ] W-2 form for this year

- [ ] Year-end pay stubs
- [ ] Any other types of income received, including sales of property even if no reporting form is received

✓ ➤ Homeowner/Renter Data

- [ ] **Mortgage interest: Form 1098**
- [ ] **Mortgage interest not reported on Form 1098.** (name and tax identification number or Social Security number)
- [ ] **Moving expenses**
- [ ] **Real estate taxes paid**
- [ ] **Rent paid during tax year if you're claiming a home-office deduction**
- [ ] **Residential address(es) for this year**
- [ ] **Sale of your home or other real estate: Form 1099-S** (if applicable and all records of purchase and sale, even if 1099-S not received such as closing statements and a list of the cost of improvements)
- [ ] **Second mortgage interest paid**

✓ ➤ Financial Data

- [ ] **Auto loans and leases if vehicles were used for business** (account numbers and car value)
- [ ] **Dividend income statements: Forms 1099-DIV**
- [ ] **Early withdrawal penalties on CDs and other time deposits: Forms 1099-INT and 1099-OID**
- [ ] **Interest income statements: Forms 1099-INT and 1099-OID**
- [ ] **IRAs, 401(k)s, other retirement plan distributions: Forms 1099-R**
- [ ] **Personal property tax information**
- [ ] **Proceeds from broker transactions: Forms 1099-B**
- [ ] **Student loan interest paid: Form 1098-E**

✓ ━━━━━━━━━━━━━━━━━━━━━━━━━━━━━━━━━━━━━▶ **Expenses**

- [ ] **Adoption expenses**
- [ ] **Alimony paid and ex-spouse's Social Security number**
- [ ] **Child and dependent care expenses**
- [ ] **Domestic employee expenses other than child care**
- [ ] **Education expenses**
- [ ] **Gifts to charity** (written statements from charities for any single donation of $250 or more)
- [ ] **Investment expenses** (see Chapter 6 for list)
- [ ] **Job-hunting expenses**
- [ ] **Medical expense records**
- [ ] **Medical savings accounts**
- [ ] **Mileage records for medical and charitable use of your car**
- [ ] **Tax return expenses and fees** (professional preparation fees, software, publications, and costs to contest an IRS decision)
- [ ] **Tuition payments for higher education: Form 1098-T**
- [ ] **Unreimbursed expenses related to volunteer work**
- [ ] **Unreimbursed expenses related to your job** (travel and transportation, uniforms, union dues, subscriptions, etc.)

✓ ━━━━━━━━━━━━━━━━━━━━━━━━━━━━━━━━━━━━━▶ **Self-Employment Data**

- [ ] **Business income: Forms 1099-MISC and/or other records**
- [ ] **Business-related expenses** (receipts, canceled checks, credit card records, other documents and records)
- [ ] **Employment taxes and other business taxes paid for current year** (payment records)
- [ ] **Farm-related income and expenses: Forms 1099-G and 1099-PATR** (receipts, other documents and records)

→ Miscellaneous Tax Documents

- ☑
- ☐ **Casualty or theft loss records or documentation**
- ☐ **Federal, state, and local estimated income tax paid for current year** (vouchers, canceled checks, and other payment records)
- ☐ **Gambling loss records**
- ☐ **IRA, SEP, and other retirement plan contributions** (If self-employed, identify if for self or employees)
- ☐ **Prior-year federal, state, and local tax balance due paid this year** (canceled checks and other payment records)
- ☐ **Records for any other expenditures that may be deductible**

Make It Easy on Yourself

smart step

Using the services of a good tax professional can save you time and money.

To avoid being "taxed" physically during the preparation of your return, make it as easy as possible on yourself. Pick your personal tax day well in advance and plan to have a successful preparation experience. You've worked all year to implement your tax plan, and now it's just a matter of finishing off the paperwork.

If your tax professional is preparing your return, call early and schedule your appointment in advance to make sure you get the day and time you want. You'll beat the rush and receive your refund sooner than if you wait until the last minute, when appointments tend to get booked up. Use your tax preparation checklist to collect all the tax-related records your tax professional will need to prepare your return. Go to your appointment, and he or she will take it from there.

Cover All Your Bases

When your tax return has been prepared, review it to make sure nothing is missing. If your tax professional prepared your tax return, he
or she should review it in detail with you. This is another opportunity for you to ask questions and explore how best to implement your tax plan
for next year if your circumstances change. If you prepared your tax return yourself, you'll need to do this review yourself. Regardless of who prepared your tax
return, you should thoroughly review and understand it before sending it to the
IRS. Here are some key items to review:

Social Security Number—A common error is incorrect or missing Social Security numbers. Without your Social Security number—or with an invalid number—the IRS won't process your return. Be sure your name and Social Security
number are on each page of your tax return for identification purposes. If
you're married and filing jointly, the first Social Security number on page one of
the return should generally be shown on the other pages of the return. You
must also provide a valid Social Security number for each of your dependents.
The IRS will disallow the exemption—and any applicable credits—for any
dependent for whom you don't provide a valid number.

Filing Status—The wrong filing status could cost you plenty. Make sure only one
filing status is checked. Checking more than one will delay the processing of your
return as the IRS attempts to find out which status is correct. The IRS might call
you or use other information on the return to decide for you, or it might send
your return back to you as not filed, creating the potential for late filing penalties.

Exemptions—Make sure the number of exemptions (the total for yourself,
your spouse, and your dependents) is correct.

Rounding—Rounding off to whole dollars reduces the risk of error and is the method the IRS prefers. You must be consistent, though; round all amounts or none. If you choose to use whole dollars, round each amount up from 50 to 99 cents, down from 49 cents or less. For example, round $10,499.50 up to $10,500, and round $10,499.49 down to $10,499.

Additional Forms—If you're including additional IRS forms with your Form 1040 or 1040A, make sure they are in the correct order. This might appear to be a minor point. But delivering the forms in sequential order makes it easier for the IRS to process your return, with less risk of missing supporting forms. Also, be sure to attach all required information forms including your W-2s and any form (such as 1099-R) that shows tax withholding.

Payment Due—Make your check (or money order) payable to the United States Treasury. Write on your check (or money order) your name, address, and daytime phone number (if not preprinted), as well as your Social Security number and the year and type of return ("2002 Form 1040," for example). Enclose your check or money order with your return. Do not staple the check to your return. If you file Form 1040, the IRS requests that you also complete and enclose Form 1040-V, Payment Voucher.

Signature—Did you sign the return? If you are married and filing jointly, did your spouse sign it, too? It seems like an obvious point, but the failure to sign a return is a common taxpayer miscue.

Keep Your Records Filed—Make sure you don't discard important documents (see Chapter 2 for more on record keeping). They don't take up that much space, and it's better to be safe than sorry. You also want to keep records sufficient to back up every entry on your return.

fast fact

If the amount you owe is less than $1, you don't have to pay it.

Owe More Taxes?

The good news is that your tax return was prepared with a minimum of fuss. Perhaps you even have a refund coming, which you can choose to receive by mail or direct deposit to your bank account. You can even get a loan for the refund amount (less fees) if you're in a hurry.

If you are not getting a loan and have a balance due, there are a number of ways to pay your tax bill. Personal checks, money orders, credit cards, and direct debit from your bank account are all accepted methods of paying your taxes. Here's a snapshot of each:

Personal Checks—Most people pay by check. If you pay by check, don't forget to sign it (a common mistake). Include your name, address, daytime phone number, Social Security number, and the year and type of the return on the face of the check.

Direct Debit Payment—If you file your return electronically, you can permit the IRS to make a direct debit from your checking or savings account. If you use this payment method, first inquire whether your financial institution handles direct debits. If it does, you must specify a date for the debit to be processed (not later than April 15) and provide the IRS with your account number and the institution's routing transit number. The process is quick and easy, and you get a confirmation notice from your bank when the debit has been made. There's another bonus: You can file early if you like, but avoid paying early. Just specify that you want to use April 15 as the date for your direct debit.

Credit Card—Whether you file your return by mail or electronically, you may use most major credit cards to pay your balance due. If you do this, write the confirmation number you are given and the tax payment amount in the upper left corner of page 1 of your tax return. American Express, MasterCard, Discover, and VISA all participate in this program. The credit card company will likely charge a convenience fee. When you file in 2003, you can inquire whether the card you want to use is accepted, the amount of the service provider's fees, and other details. You can obtain information and charge your taxes by calling 1-800-2PAY-TAX or 1-888-PAY-1040, or via the Internet at www.officialpayments.com or www.PAY1040.com.

The Installment Plan

If you are caught off guard by an unexpected tax bill, the IRS may work with you to set up an installment plan. You can apply by completing Form 9465 and attaching it to your tax return. You should get a response in about thirty days. If you get the thumbs-up from Uncle Sam, the agreement will cover the tax balance due and any interest and penalties you owe, plus a user fee. You will be required to make monthly payments on time and in full as called for in the installment plan, or the IRS may cancel the agreement. The IRS can deny your request for several reasons, including if during the past few years, you have entered into an installment agreement for payment of your tax liability.

Because the late payment penalty (up to 25 percent of the tax owed) and interest continue to accrue during the installment period, obtaining (if possible) a bank line of credit or loan may be a wiser choice than an installment plan. If you need just a little time to pay the amount you owe, paying by credit card or getting a cash advance from your credit card may be best. Your tax professional can estimate the cost of each of these options.

fast fact

You can file electronically, sign your return electronically, and even get your refund or pay your balance due electronically.

THE CHALLENGE

Brent, a business development consultant, made his living by working with large corporations. But the consulting industry had slumped in a down economy, and it was no longer the goose laying the golden eggs. When the thirty-six-year-old found that his business had dried up quicker than a summer rainstorm in Texas, and his cash along with it, he knew that he might be in trouble. To make matters worse, it was tax time, and he already knew he had a balance due.

THE PLAN

Brent looked around on his own, then made a quick call to his tax professional who explained that he had more options than he thought. He could pay the bill by credit card, apply to enter into an installment plan with the IRS, or even draw on his home equity line of credit. "My tax professional explained why I shouldn't tap my retirement account because of the high tax penalties," he said. "I was going to charge my tax bill, but really couldn't face the prospect of maxing out my credit card at a fairly high interest rate. I liked the installment plan, but I didn't like the thought of the fees, interest, and penalties." Brent quickly concluded that his home equity line of credit, which carried a 5 percent rate of interest, was the best choice for him. "I'd originally gotten it to build a home office for my business," he said. "Once the construction was finished, I paid off the loan after my first consulting job." Having made his decision, Brent wrote the check, promptly settling his account with Uncle Sam. "Writing that check was one of the hardest things I have had to do," he said. "But it's good to know that I had options."

e-Filing

The IRS and e-filing providers have worked hard to make e-filing easy and safe, and millions of Americans are switching to this fast, safe, and dependable option. One of the main benefits is that they receive their refunds faster, which only makes the paperwork reduction and fast transmittal nice fringe benefits.

Other benefits of the e-route? Filing electronically ensures that your return can't be lost in the mail: you'll get an acknowledgment that the IRS received your tax return. E-filing does not increase your odds of an IRS audit (nor does it decrease them). In addition, e-filing reduces the risk of processing errors. Most likely, you can also electronically file your state income tax return, but check with your state to be sure.

To enjoy the benefits of filing electronically, you are required to file through an e-file provider authorized by the IRS. Generally, providers will charge a fee for this service. To use this service, you can:

- **Have your return prepared and filed electronically by your tax professional or authorized e-file provider.** Make sure your tax professional offers e-filing.
- **Prepare your return with tax preparation software** (you'll need Internet access to e-file) **or use an online tax program and select electronic filing of the completed return** (discussed in Chapter 12).
- **Prepare your return on paper then take it to an authorized e-file provider for electronic filing.**

The majority of e-filed tax returns are received and accepted by the IRS without any issues or problems. However, sometimes an error will cause your e-filed

smart step

To receive a quicker refund and avoid processing errors, file your return electronically.

return to be rejected. If this occurs, your provider will notify you and assist you with the correction process. If your return was rejected because of a misspelled name or an incorrect Social Security number or birth date, the errors can be fixed and the return resubmitted to the IRS. More complex rejection problems may require that you file a paper tax return. Make sure your e-file provider explains what you need to do and the deadline for filing the paper tax return to have it counted as filed on time.

If you must file a paper tax return because of a rejection error, be sure to print and attach a copy of your rejection message to your tax return and write "TIMELY FILED REJECTED ELECTRONIC RETURN" across the top of your paper tax return.

The U.S. Postal Service Still Delivers

If filing your tax return electronically makes you uncomfortable, you can still mail it. You can use certified mail and may want to consider doing so if you are filing close to the deadline or have a balance due. It costs only a few extra dollars, and if that gives you peace of mind, then it's worth it.

If you are sending a check to the IRS, or if you are making an election that the law says has to be made by the due date, a certified mail receipt proves the date you mailed—and you are thus considered to have filed—your return. A dated receipt from a qualified private delivery service will also be accepted by the IRS as proof that your return was filed on time. Note that not all private delivery services qualify. You can find a list of qualified services in the Form 1040 instruction booklet.

Filing for an Extension

I f you need more time, you can file Form 4868 by April 15 to get an automatic four-month extension to file your tax return. The form is available from the IRS Web site, your tax professional, and in many software and online preparation programs. You can file Form 4868 by telephone or electronically. You should file for an extension whether you have a balance due or are expecting a refund.

An extension of time to file is not an extension of time to pay. You must estimate your tax liability when you prepare Form 4868 and remit any expected balance due with the form. If you haven't paid at least 90 percent of your tax bill by April 15, a late payment penalty may apply. An extension will be granted even if the balance due is not paid in full. If mailed, your extension must be postmarked by midnight, April 15.

smart step

Avoid penalties and interest by paying your full tax when you apply for an extension to file your return.

Extension Filing Guidelines

- **File Form 4868, Application for Automatic Extension of Time to File U.S. Individual Income Tax Return, on or before the regular due date of your tax return, normally April 15.** You can mail the form, file online, or file by telephone. The number to call is on the form. Check to see if you need to file a separate state form to receive an extension for filing your state tax return.
- **Pay at least 90 percent of the tax due through withholding or estimated tax payments either before the original due date of your tax return or with your extension.** If you don't, you will face late payment penalties.
- **Avoid interest charges by paying the entire amount of tax due on your tax return by April 15, even if you are filing an extension.**

Filing for an extension of time to file doesn't give you more time to pay. To avoid a late-payment penalty, you must pay at least 90 percent of your taxes by April 15.

Abide by your new due date of August 15 after you file your extension Form 4868. A second extension period is available by filing Form 2688, Application for Additional Extension of Time To File U.S. Individual Income Tax Return, which would make your new due date October 15. This is not an automatic extension, and you must have a good reason for needing the additional time. The IRS may deny your request, so you should allow extra time so you can file your tax return by August 15 in case the IRS denies your request.

Check to see if you need to file a separate state form to get an extension for filing your state tax return.

It's April 16—and You Forgot to File

Oops! Did you forget to file your tax return by April 15? Don't delay any longer! First and foremost, file immediately, even if you owe and can't pay. A tax professional can help you get this done quickly.

If you are not able to pay your tax liability by April 15 you will need to seek out other options right away:

- **Pay what you can immediately**
- **Enter into a formal installment agreement with the IRS** (requires IRS approval)
- **Pay by credit card or get a loan to pay what you owe**

Don't waste time. Take immediate action to correct this situation because the stakes increase quickly. If you neglect to file your return or extension request by April 15 and you owe taxes, you will be hit with a failure to file penalty plus interest compounded daily on the taxes due, starting from April 15. If you drag your feet too much, the IRS can eventually take payments from your wages and put liens on your property.

Filing an Amended Return

What happens if you filed your tax return and later discover that you made an error, forgot a key deduction, or missed a tax credit? Fortunately, you're not out of luck: That's why the IRS created the amended tax return. Formally known as Form 1040X, it allows you to right some wrongs on your completed and filed tax return.

The IRS service center that processes your tax return normally corrects obvious errors, such as math errors, and requests information such as Social Security numbers and forms (such as W-2s) and schedules you left out. In these instances, don't worry about amending your tax return. Simply—and promptly—submit the requested information to the contact identified on the notice that you receive from the IRS.

That said, you *do* need to file an amended tax return if any of the following were reported incorrectly:

■ **Your tax payments**
■ **Your deductions or credits**
■ **Your total income**
■ **Your filing status**
■ **Any other items that affect the bottom line of your tax return**

smart
step

If you can't pay your taxes by April 15, file your return and pay what you can. The IRS will bill you for the rest, including interest and a late-payment penalty, but you will escape the late-filing penalty.

More specifically, some items that could create the problems listed above include:

- **Changing your filing status**
- **Errors in computing deductions or credits on the original return**
- **Failure to report or underreporting some income**
- **Not claiming exemptions, deductions, or credits to which you are entitled, or claiming items for which you don't qualify**
- **Understating or overstating your tax payments**

You should also file an amended return if you made a mathematical error on a form or a worksheet that is not attached to your tax return, if the error changes your tax liability.

How Do I File an Amended Return?

If you need to correct a tax return, you can attempt it on your own or work with your tax professional to complete Form 1040X, Amended U.S. Individual Income Tax Return. Be sure to provide the required explanation of the changes and attach any reporting forms such as W-2s you did not include with your original tax return. You'll also need to include forms and schedules for any new income, deductions, or credits not reported on the original return, and a copy of any other forms or schedules that changed as a result of the changes you made. You do not need to send a copy of your original tax return. In most instances, Form 1040X must be filed within three years of the date you filed the original tax return or within two years after the date you paid the tax, whichever is later. Note that an original tax return filed before the due date is considered filed on April 15.

Special Filing Situations

I f you're a United States citizen and you live outside the United States and Puerto Rico on April 15, you have the same filing requirements as any other citizen. However, you get an automatic, two-month extension to complete and file your tax return. Plus, you can get the additional two months until August 15 by filing for Form 4868.

The same rule applies to United States military men and women on duty outside the United States and Puerto Rico. If you're a civilian, both your residence and tax home must be outside the United States and Puerto Rico.

Citizens living abroad in these situations use the same tax forms they'd use if they'd lived stateside. However, you are more likely to be eligible to claim a foreign tax credit, and if you work in a foreign country, you may qualify for the limited exclusion of foreign earned income. To claim the credit and exclusion, complete Forms 1116 and 2555, respectively, and attach them to your tax return. Be aware that the credit and exclusion cannot both be claimed for the same income. You may need to turn to your tax professional for assistance.

smart step

If you live outside the U.S., ask your tax professional about the foreign tax credit and foreign income exclusion. Either could save you money.

Tax Return Mistakes

Here are some common mistakes people make on their tax returns. Any one of these errors could cause the processing of your return and the receipt of any refund to be delayed by an additional eight weeks or more.

Dependency Exemptions—Make sure the names and Social Security numbers for your dependents are accurate before filing your return. The IRS will deny the exemption until you provide the correct information. Having the wrong

fast fact

To check the status of an amended tax return, contact the IRS assistance line at 800-829-1040. It can take up to twelve weeks or longer to process an amended tax return.

Social Security numbers on your Form 1040 can affect a variety of exemptions and credits, such as the child tax credit, the child-care credit, and the earned income credit.

Earned income credit errors—A common error is the claiming of this credit by taxpayers who aren't eligible for it. Review the eligibility requirements carefully. Errors in the computation of the credit also occur frequently.

Missing information—Forgetting to include Forms W-2 and 1099 will delay the processing of your return.

Social Security number—If your Social Security number or your spouse's is incorrect or illegible it will cause processing problems and bring things to a stop until the correct number is provided.

Child tax credit—If you are the parent of a child or children under age 17, you may qualify for a nonrefundable credit of up to $600 per child. You may also qualify for the refundable additional child tax credit computed on Form 8812. This latter credit is often overlooked.

Social Security benefits—Retirees sometimes find it difficult to determine how much of their Social Security benefits are subject to tax. Miscalculating the taxable amount may cause you to pay more tax than is necessary.

Refund amount or amount due—Math errors and misunderstanding the tax table and schedules often lead to this common problem.

Filing status—Choosing an incorrect filing status, or even a "correct" but less than optimal filing status, can cost you a lot of money. See Chapter 3 and the IRS instructions for Form 1040 to make sure you're using the best filing status for you.

the ESSENTIALS

1 Create a checklist for all the items you're going to need to complete your tax return.

2 The IRS provides you with options to pay your tax liability due: personal check or money order, bank account debit (if you e-file), or credit card.

3 e-Filing your tax return is a fast, safe, and dependable alternative to mailing your return.

4 You can receive an automatic four-month extension to file your tax return. However, this is not an extension of time to pay your tax liability.

5 If you need to correct a mistake on a filed tax return, you can file an amended tax return.

fast fact

You cannot send an amended tax return electronically. You must complete Form 1040X and mail it to your IRS service center.

11 [FEAR NOT: How to Avoid an IRS Audit]

"If it wasn't for the honor, I'd just as soon skip the whole thing."
—A man about to be publicly hanged

To be prepared
for an audit,
keep all docu-
ments related
to your return
for at least
three years
after the date
you file your re-
turn.

An IRS audit is inconvenient and not particularly pleasant, but it isn't the end of the world. If you've completed your return honestly and have records to back up your income, deductions, and credits, you'll come out of the experience with a little wear and tear on your nerves, but financially intact. There is even an upside: During the process, you may find some tax breaks that you missed the first time around and actually come out ahead.

In this chapter, we'll provide you with some tips for avoiding audits and some advice about what to do if you receive that IRS letter. However you feel about audits, don't let the thought of one deter you from taking any legal deductions or credits for which you're eligible and that you can document. Doing so is like burning perfectly good cash in your fireplace.

What Is a Tax Audit?

Strictly speaking, a tax audit is an IRS examination and verification of your tax return. The IRS conducts three types of tax audits:

- **Correspondence Audits**—Returns with one or a few routine questions are handled by tax examiners via mail or telephone from the IRS service center where the return was filed. The IRS counts only the more complex of these contacts in its number-of-audit statistics.

- **Office Audits**—An audit involving more numerous or complex issues will normally take place in a meeting with a tax auditor at an IRS office.

- **Field Audits**—A business tax return, including a self-employed individual's return, may face a field audit conducted by an IRS revenue agent at the taxpayer's business premises or in the office of the tax professional representing the taxpayer.

You should also know about three other divisions of the IRS. Contact the Appeals Division if you ever decide to appeal an audit decision. You may hear from the Collections Division if you don't pay an assessed tax (plus interest and penalties) and fail to respond to the resulting notices from Collections. The Criminal Investigation Division is one you don't ever want to face. If a **Special Agent** ever contacts you, consult a tax attorney immediately.

The percentage of tax returns the IRS audits that are counted as audits is currently quite small and the agency strives to improve its selection process. The IRS uses various methods to target returns. Among the most common are computer identification of items that are often reported incorrectly, or that seem to be abnormal in relation to other items on the return, the earned income credit, entries on the miscellaneous income line, and document matching that compares W-2s and other reporting forms received by the IRS with income reported on the return.

Some returns are selected through a DIF (discriminate function) score process. Using this program, all individual tax returns are scored according to items reported on the return. All returns with DIF scores above a cutoff score are reviewed—that is, classified—manually to decide which ones will be selected for examination, what issues will be examined, and what type of audit will be conducted.

Generally, the IRS can't audit a return more than three years after it is filed. In most cases, you're home free if you don't get an audit notice within about twenty months after you file your return. But there are exceptions: If unreported income exceeds 25 percent of the gross income reported on the return, the audit period increases to six years, and in the case of taxpayer fraud the period extends forever.

plain talk

Special Agents are law enforcement officers who investigate financial crimes associated with tax evasion, money laundering, narcotics, organized crime, public corruption, and more.

Is Filing Late—or Early—An Audit Shield?

Whether you file your return early or late in the filing season does not affect the chance of your tax return being selected for an audit. The IRS puts all returns through the same process. Computer programs and other outside sources are used to identify returns that may have incorrect amounts and are, therefore, more likely to be audited. Because your chances of being audited are remote anyway, don't worry about trying to find the magic date that will prevent an audit. Instead, file a complete and accurate return as soon as it's ready, and keep detailed records in case you wind up being audited.

You may feel a little uneasy about the prospect of an audit, but remember the IRS examines returns all of the time. Let's take a look at some items that may trigger a tax audit.

Potential Audit Triggers

Common sense should tell you what audit triggers or red flags to avoid. For instance, if you report only $10,000 of wages but your Form W-2 shows $50,000, that's a problem. Warnings bells might sound if you claimed that 50 percent of your income went to charity. To help avoid an audit, you should give specific attention to items the IRS will review.

Charitable Contributions—If you make generous contributions to charities and religious organizations, you should keep a log of your donations. You should note the date, the name and address of the organization, and the amount of the contribution you made. To provide backup for your log, pay by check or credit card when such a payment method is practical. If you contribute

$250 or more at one time, a written receipt from the organization is also required. You must obtain this receipt before the earlier of the date you file your return or the return's due date (including extensions). If asked, some charitable organizations will issue you a receipt for your contribution even if it is for a small amount. Remember to keep track of and deduct your out-of-pocket expenses for volunteer work.

If you donate clothes and household items to a charity, ask for a receipt. This document should include the name and address of the organization, the date of the donation, and a reasonably detailed description of the property. Make a list of the items and the fair market value of each item at the time of the donation; this is essential if your property is worth more than $500. If total property donations are more than $500, you must also file Form 8283 with your return. With few exceptions, you must obtain and usually attach to your return a written appraisal from a qualified appraiser for any item, or group of similar items, valued at more than $5,000. The larger your donation, the more the IRS scrutinizes it.

Dependency Exemptions—A dependency exemption will be disallowed if the dependent's full name and Social Security number on your return doesn't match the IRS data. During an audit, you may be asked to provide evidence that your dependents pass the five tests we discussed in Chapter 3: gross income test; support test; member of household or relationship test; citizenship or residence test; and joint return test.

Higher Income —As your income increases, generally so do your odds of being audited, especially if you have income from rentals, businesses, or other sources that isn't reported on an information return such as a W-2 or 1099. Your protection? As always, keep an "as you receive it" log to record the date and amount for all income you receive.

fast
fact

The IRS receives a copy of each Form W-2 and 1099 that you receive, so be sure to report income correctly.

ACTUAL PERCENTAGE OF RETURNS AUDITED	
INCOME	% OF RETURNS AUDITED
INDIVIDUAL RETURNS WITH NO BUSINESS INCOME:	
$25,000 to less than $50,000	0.21
$50,000 to less than $100,000	0.23
$100,000 and over	0.84
INDIVIDUAL RETURNS WITH SCHEDULE C:	
Under $25,000	2.69
$25,000 to under $100,000	1.30
$100,000 and over	2.40

Source: IRS statistical data for audits of 1999 individual tax returns through September 2000.

Home Office and Other Business Expenses—If you are self-employed or an employee and take deductions for a home office or other expenses, be aware that the IRS often reviews deductions for expenses that could be either business or personal.

If you deduct home-office expenses, make sure you meet the requirements discussed in Chapter 8. Make an accurate determination of the portion of your home used as an office, most commonly the ratio of the square footage of the business space to the total square footage of your home. Keep records of repairs, maintenance, and any other items related to the office, as well as your utility bills, with your tax records for the year. In addition to receipts and canceled checks, make a note of the business purpose of each deductible expense. Should you move, take pictures of the home office and keep the photo and records of the size of the home with your tax records.

Another area for exercising extraordinary diligence is record keeping for travel, meals, and entertainment. These deductions fall into the high-error-potential class in the IRS audit selection process. In addition, tax law mandates specific standards for documenting these expenses because of the relative ease of co-mingling personal and business expenses, either deliberately or through honest error. Local transportation expenses also fall in this category. Numerous self-employed individuals and employees claim legitimate deductions for expenses of operating a vehicle that is used for both personal and business purposes. These deductions, computed using a mileage allowance or actual expenses, need to be backed by complete records of business mileage and the purpose and destination, as well as the total mileage for the year. Receipts and records of the total amount of actual expenses are also required if you claim these expenses instead of the mileage allowance. In addition, you will want to be able to show that any business or employment-related deductions you claim are ordinary and necessary expenses of the activity.

As shown by the chart on the preceding page, returns containing Schedule C, the business return for self-employed individuals, are audited more often, especially if they report income of $100,000 or more, or less than $25,000 (including those reporting losses).

Unreported Alimony—The IRS is quite aware that some alimony payers don't pay but deduct anyway and some recipients receive and don't report. Therefore, the ex-spouse's Social Security number is required on the payer's return. Omitting this number will result in a delay in the processing of the return and may result in a disallowance of the deduction.

Unreported Income—Spells trouble! If you neglect to report income that has been reported on an information return, the IRS is very successful at finding it. The IRS matches nearly 100 percent of the W-2s and 1099s it receives against the returns on which the income should be reported. This type of discrepancy is typical of the audits handled by correspondence from the service center—and these aren't counted as audits in the IRS's statistics. It also has various investigative methods to track down other unreported income that comes to its attention.

smart step

If you donate a vehicle to charity, you can generally deduct the smaller of your basis in the vehicle or its fair market value when donated. Be sure to value it accurately—typically, the amount you could get if you sold it.

smart step

Take all the tax breaks to which you're entitled, even if they appear on our list of potential audit triggers. Your chances of being audited are still small, and if your records are complete you don't need to fear an audit.

- **Business meal and entertainment deductions** (excessive)
- **Business transportation deductions** (excessive)
- **Casualty losses** (large)
- **Charitable contribution deductions** (non-cash)
- **Earned income credit**
- **Exemptions** (especially dependents who aren't your children or who don't live with you)
- **Higher levels of income**
- **Home-office deduction** (especially if your business shows a loss)
- **Itemized deductions** (excessive)
- **Large business, rental, or farm losses**
- **Unreported income** (that has been reported to the IRS)

Avoiding an IRS Audit

In addition to knowing what may trigger an audit, take these additional steps to reduce the odds of the IRS selecting and scrutinizing your return.

Documents and Receipts—The only documents you should normally attach to your tax return are your W-2s and any 1099s or other income information forms that report federal tax withheld. Never attach original receipts or other proof documents unless they are specifically required by the IRS. If you must send the IRS a document—for example, an appraisal for the contribution of property valued at more than $5,000—obtain a certified or notarized copy for your records (or, preferably, send it to the IRS).

THE CHALLENGE

Jillian never intended to be misleading on her tax return; she was just too focused on running her new business. The twenty-seven year-old graphic artist had recently started a design business in a studio she converted from the loft above her garage. "I didn't really pay much attention to taxes, other than a little reading on self-employment taxes."

About a year later, while looking for a check in the mail, Jillian received an IRS notice indicating that her tax return for her first year of business was being audited. "I was scared," Jillian recalled. "I had no idea how to defend myself at an audit."

THE PLAN

Jillian immediately called a tax professional who told her to bring the notice over to her office so they could discuss it. After thoroughly reviewing the audit notice, the tax professional spotted the problem. Jillian had taken two trips to graphic-design seminars—one to Arizona, and the other to Louisiana during the period of the audit inquiry. The IRS needed verification that these trips were for business and not personal. The tax professional advised her to find the credit card receipts for her travel expenses and fees for the two seminars she had attended. "She asked me to get the brochures and agendas from the seminars and make copies of everything," Jillian explained. "She also had me describe in writing how the seminars benefited my business. Finally, she advised me to sign a Form 2848, Power of Attorney, so she could represent me." A few weeks after she sent the requested information to the IRS, Jillian received another notice telling her that her audit was resolved successfully.

Jillian learned some valuable lessons. "I've set up a filing system to maintain my business expense receipts and other documents, along with the purpose of expenses that might be questioned. In addition, I opened a separate business checking account, and I have a credit card to use strictly for business. This will make it easier to document my business income and expenses. I'm going to be ready and unafraid of audits from now on."

Measure Twice, Cut Once—The same principle applies to the math on your return. If you prepare your return manually, make sure your math is correct. Errors involving arithmetic are among the most common found by the IRS.

Organized Records—Maintaining adequate tax and financial records has been a recurring theme in this book. Coming away from an audit with no damage is an excellent incentive to organize your records. If you maintain accurate and detailed tax and financial records, you'll know where you stand financially, be better able to plan your future, and will be able to substantiate the information on your return if you're audited.

Required Information—Be sure to enter all required information on your return, including Social Security numbers and other taxpayer ID numbers, and double check to see that they are correct. Compare the income and expenses reported on your return with the original documents and your records to be sure you have no errors or omissions. Attach an explanation and computation of the amount for items that may raise questions, including items entered on the miscellaneous income line.

Round Off Your Numbers—Rounding to whole dollars is easier for most taxpayers. It reduces the risk of error and is the method the IRS prefers. Round each amount up from 50 to 99 cents, down from 49 cents or less. For example, $10,499.50 is rounded up to $10,500, while $10,499.49 is rounded down to $10,499. You must be consistent, though, and round off all amounts or none.

Use a Computer—If you do it yourself, a computer-prepared return is faster and easier to prepare. It should be error-free arithmetically and would be appreciated by the IRS. In addition, the software typically allows you to e-file your return.

What's Average?

Some people wonder what an average tax return looks like. The table below is a look at the average amount of specific itemized deductions for taxpayers who itemized. Do not, however, think the statistics make it safe for you to claim more than you have, and don't claim less than your actual amounts either. Both actions are potential money losers.

AVERAGE TAX RETURNS			
YEARLY INCOME	DEDUCTIBLE TAXES	DEDUCTIBLE INTEREST	CHARITABLE CONTRIBUTIONS
$30–49,999	$3,026	$6,422	$1,895
$50–99,999	$4,899	$7,828	$2,349
$100–199,999	$9,283	$11,161	$3,761
$200+	$38,200	$22,598	$19,559

Source: Treasury Dept. Statistics of Income Bulletin, Winter 2001-2002

smart step

Double-check that all Social Security numbers for your dependents, yourself, and your spouse are correct before your return is filed.

Responding to An Audit

This is the letter you don't want to receive:

Dear Taxpayer,
Some of the information that you provided to us does not agree with the information we received from other sources. Please contact us at 1-800-XXX-XXXX for further review of your tax records.
Cordially,
The Internal Revenue Service

Everybody likes to get mail, unless it's a Dear John letter or a note from Uncle Sam, like the one shown above. If you receive one of these letters from Uncle

smart step

If your audit involves more than simply sending the IRS some requested document, consult a tax professional before responding to the IRS.

Sam (you're on your own with the other one), try to relax. The IRS is staffed with regular people. They have a job to do: the need to verify the accuracy of your return. When you file a complete and accurate return and can back up your income, deductions, and credits, you have nothing to worry about. However, you do have options if you should happen to run into a rare bad apple.

Everyone makes mistakes, including the IRS. So if you are the unlucky recipient of an audit notice, carefully look for the following items:

Is your name, address, and Social Security number on the notice?—The notice may be for another taxpayer with a similar name, or the postal service may have delivered it to the wrong address.

Can the inquiry be handled by mail?—If the notice requests information rather than giving a date for an office audit, you can handle the process by answering the questions, providing copies of the appropriate back-up documentation, and mailing your response as directed in the notice.

Has the statute of limitations expired?—In most cases, the IRS must begin an audit within three years of the date you file your return for the year being examined. Returns filed before April 15 are considered filed on April 15.

After you have scanned the letter for the criteria above, you should consider the following:

You may need a professional—Contact a tax professional right away if you have any doubts about how to respond to an IRS audit notice, even with a correspondence audit. Getting help is especially necessary if the IRS has disallowed an exemption, deduction, or credit, or has added income that you believe you already reported or never received. It is essential to respond promptly to an IRS notice, but it is also essential to respond accurately and to defend your return when it is correct. A professional can go over the notice and your return with you, and deal with the IRS if you wish, or explain what you need to do.

You can have reasonable say in the place and time of the audit—Be aware that you have the right to request a transfer of a service center audit to an office audit, and you may also reschedule an office or field audit to a time that works for you, as long as you don't unreasonably delay the proceeding. Rescheduling, when necessary, gives you time to organize your records and allows your tax professional time to review your records prior to the audit.

You can run, but you can't hide—Moving won't stop an audit. If you happen to move out of state after you file a tax return that the IRS selects for an audit, you can ask the IRS to move the meeting to an office closer to your new location. If your tax professional still lives in your old area, you can ask him or her to handle the audit for you. You don't have to be present at an audit if you give a tax professional a power of attorney to represent you with regard to the audit issues.

➤ If you receive an audit notice from the IRS:

- Take it seriously
- Respond promptly to the inquiry, even if the notice is received in error or after the audit period has expired
- Respond to all the issues in an inquiry, including any errors in the notice
- Consider contacting a tax professional for help in preparing for the audit or to handle the audit for you
- Request a postponement to get professional assistance if you have any doubts about how to respond
- Review the IRS proposal, and the arithmetic, before you agree to any proposed changes

Give the IRS auditor only the documents and tax forms requested and answer only the questions asked. Do not volunteer additional information or engage in idle conversation.

Mistakes and delays in your response can cost you time and money, not to mention a skyrocketing stress level.

At the Audit

As explained at the beginning of this chapter, the IRS conducts three types of audits: correspondence audits, office audits, and field audits.

A correspondence audit involves one or a few routine questions that can generally be resolved by mailing or faxing your answer and copies of requested documents.

Office audits involve more numerous or more complex questions and range from fairly cursory to very thorough. This is the type of audit to expect if the IRS questions items such as your medical or charitable deductions or your employee business expenses.

Field audits of business returns are the most arduous and thorough. During these audits, the IRS conducts an in-depth examination of the taxpayer's business books and financial records. A field audit is generally held at the taxpayer's place of business where the business books are located, or at the tax professional's office.

Our discussion will focus on office audits. Bring to the audit only the documents and records that were requested in the audit notice. If the auditor wants more data, ask him or her to put it in writing, so you have a record of what's been requested in case you appeal. Your request may also cause the auditor (who wants to close the case) to decide the information isn't needed after all.

At the conclusion of the audit, the IRS auditor will advise you of any proposed changes to your tax return. Later, the auditor will write a formal report that will be reviewed by the auditor's supervisor. If you don't agree with the auditor's findings, you can request a meeting with the supervisor, who, if available at the time, will discuss the issues with you immediately.

If you agree with the results and you owe tax, you can square your account with Uncle Sam and write a check on the spot, although it is usually advisable to wait until you receive the written report. Waiting does not increase penalties and interest if you pay within the period stated on the report. In addition, it allows time for the air to clear and for you to decide whether you have grounds to appeal or how to pay what you owe. If you can't refute the audit results and you can't pay immediately, you can take the extra time to work out a payment plan or an **offer-in-compromise** with the IRS.

Contesting Your Audit Results

If you don't agree with the final audit results, you can request a review by the Appeals Division of the IRS. An appeals officer considers the risk and the cost of litigation, as well as the facts. And, the price is right: it's free. We recommend taking this step because you have a lot to gain and little to lose. You have two alternatives to the Appeals Division:

- You can petition the Tax Court within ninety days (one hundred fifty days if outside the United States) after you receive a deficiency notice and before you pay the stated tax deficiency. The Tax Court typically sends the issue to IRS Appeals to attempt settlement before hearing the case, so it usually makes sense for you to take your case to the Appeals Division first.
  If you decide to go to Tax Court, and the contested deficiency is not more than $50,000, consider the small tax case procedure. It's inexpensive, and the process

plain talk

An offer-in-compromise occurs when a taxpayer is unable to pay the tax owed and the IRS accepts a lesser amount than is due.

is much simpler than in a regular court proceeding. You can represent yourself or you can hire an attorney. Be aware, however, that the court's decision will be final. Neither you nor the IRS can appeal a small case decision.

■ You can pay the tax due, file Form 1040X to claim a refund of tax on the disputed items, and after the IRS has denied the claim or ignored it for six months, file suit in a U.S. District Court or the Court of Federal Claims.

Pros and Cons of Appeals

To decide whether to appeal an adverse audit decision, weigh the pros and cons. Ask a tax professional to review the situation. Is your return otherwise accurate and complete? Could an appeal open prior year returns? Does tax authority exist that justifies all or part of your position or cast doubt on the IRS's stance? If you concede one issue, is it likely that an appeals officer will concede another?

The Pros—If you do your homework, you may win. The proposed tax bill, along with the interest and penalty, will disappear on any part of the appeal you win.

The Cons—It is open season on items uncovered in an audit. The IRS appeals officer may find additional items to investigate that didn't come up in the original audit. If you lose, you will owe the recomputed tax deficiency plus interest and penalties, which continue to accumulate during the process.

The IRS Appeals Office operates autonomously from the IRS's audit division, and the office has a mission to settle cases out of court if reasonably possible. To get the appeals process rolling, read IRS Publication 5, Your Appeal Rights and How to Prepare a Protest If You Don't Agree, which you will receive with the deficiency notice from the IRS. Follow the instructions provided. The more complex the issues, the wiser it is to consult a tax professional to review your situation, assess your chances, and, in many cases, handle the appeal for you.

The Taxpayer Bill of Rights

This tax law gives you specific rights in your dealings with the IRS. It was voted into law by Congress in the mid 1980s and strengthened in 1996 and 1998. Here is a summary of the Taxpayer Bill of Rights.

Privacy and Confidentiality—You have the right to have your personal and financial information kept confidential. The IRS cannot disclose your information to anyone, except as allowed by law. You also have the right to know why the IRS is asking for the information, exactly how the IRS will use any information you provide, and what might happen if you do not give the information.

Information Sharing—Under the law, the IRS can share your tax information with state tax agencies and, under strict legal guidelines, the Department of Justice and other federal agencies. The IRS can also share tax information with certain foreign governments under tax treaty provisions.

Courtesy and Consideration—You are entitled to courteous and considerate treatment from IRS employees. If you ever feel that an IRS employee is not treating you as such, tell the employee's supervisor.

fast fact

A collection officer does not generally need a court order to seize your property. But you don't have to allow the employee access to your home or non-public areas of your business if he or she does not have court authorization.

Protection of Your Rights—The employees of the IRS will explain and protect your rights as a taxpayer at all times. If you feel that this is not the case, discuss the problem with the employee's supervisor.

Complaints—If for any reason you have a complaint about the IRS, you may write to the district director or Service Center for your area. If you call the tax-payer advocate toll-free number, the IRS will give you the name and address of the appropriate district director.

Taxpayer Advocate—The taxpayer advocate's primary mission is to assist tax-payers with ongoing issues that have not been resolved through the regular IRS processes or that are causing the taxpayer to suffer significant hardships. To request assistance, you must generally file Form 911, Application for Taxpayer Assistance Order. You can reach the Taxpayer Advocate by calling toll-free 1-877-777-4778 or going through the general IRS line 1-800-829-1040. For full details, go to www.irs.gov and click on Taxpayer Advocate.

Taxpayer Interviews—Publication 1, Your Rights as a Taxpayer, is included with any audit notice. The IRS must provide a reasonable time and place for an audit and, within guidelines, grant your reasonable request for rescheduling. In addition, IRS employees must clearly explain and protect your rights throughout your contact with the IRS.

Representation—You may represent yourself, and you may request a post-ponement of the balance of an audit to consult with a tax professional. Alternatively, if you give authorization, an enrolled agent, certified public accountant, or attorney may represent you. The tax professional who prepared your return may represent you at audit, but not at Appeals or within the IRS Collections Division. Once you have authorized a professional representative, the IRS may not interview you alone without your consent, except in certain extenuating circumstances.

Recordings—You may make a sound recording of your meeting with any examination, appeal, or collection personnel by informing the IRS in writing ten days before the meeting. Similarly, the IRS may record a meeting if it gives you a ten-day written notice.

Interest—You must pay interest on any additional tax you owe, generally figured from the due date of the return. If an IRS error caused a delay in your case, and this was grossly unfair, the IRS may reduce the amount of interest.

Reliance on Written Advice—The IRS must cancel any portion of a penalty imposed on you if the error on your return is the result of a written opinion given by the IRS in response to a question you submitted and the question includes complete and accurate details about the issue.

Action for Damages—If an IRS employee intentionally disregards the tax code or regulations in collecting a tax liability, you may sue the government in federal court, although not if the disregard is in connection with determining the amount of the tax.

Lien/Levy—The IRS may place a lien on your property as security for a tax debt that you haven't arranged to pay. If deemed necessary for collection, the IRS may levy (legally seize) your property, including wages and bank accounts, although not until thirty days after it notifies you of the planned seizure. However, it cannot levy and sell your property if the expense of doing so would exceed either the property's fair market value or the amount of the tax deficiency.

Property Exempt from Levy—If the IRS levies your property, you have the legal right to keep the following:

- **A limited amount of personal belongings, furniture, and business or professional books and tools**

fast fact

There is certain property the IRS can't take from you regardless of the amount of tax you owe.

smart
step

Know your
rights before
dealing with
any government
agency.

- School books and certain clothing
- Your main house and tangible personal property or real property used in your trade or business unless collection of tax is in jeopardy or the district director (or assistant) approves the levy in writing
- The income you need to pay court-ordered child support
- Unemployment and job training benefits, workers' compensation, public assistance payments, certain disability payments, and certain pension benefits
- Undelivered mail
- Weekly wages or other income equal to your standard deduction and allowable personal and dependency exemptions, divided by 52
- If the amount of levy is $5,000 or less, any real property used as your residence, or any other non-rental real property

Joint Returns—The IRS is required to disclose collection activities on joint returns to former spouses, upon written request.

Change of Filing Status—Married taxpayers may switch their filing status from married filing separately to married filing jointly without first paying the tax due on the separate returns that will not be due on a joint return.

Generally, you will find the IRS personnel to be courteous. In almost all cases, they respect taxpayers' rights. Still, it's smart to enter any dealings with any government agency with a basic knowledge of your rights.

the ESSENTIALS

1 The IRS conducts audits to clear up discrepancies, check for compliance in selected issues, and verify the completeness and accuracy of selected returns.

2 The best way to avoid an audit is to double-check your return to ensure it is complete and accurate before you file it. You should also maintain adequate records to document your income, exemptions, deductions, credits, and tax payments.

3 A smart move to reduce stress—and come out of an audit with minimal or no damage—is to ask a tax professional to handle an audit for you.

4 The Taxpayer Bill of Rights guarantees specific rights in your dealings with the IRS.

12 [DO IT THE e-WAY: A Look at Electronic Options]

"If necessity is the mother of invention, then resourcefulness is the father."
—Beulah Louise Henry

Selecting
e-filing as the
method of fil-
ing your return
does not affect
your chances of
being audited.

As the story goes, Henry uttered these words in reference to her invention, a new type of umbrella with snap-on covers. Perhaps it wasn't a big advance in terms of technology (although the umbrella manufacturers of the time claimed it couldn't be done), but the umbrella was handy during a downpour, and fashionable, too.

Over the years, inventions have changed—and continue to change—our everyday lives. In the past, people had to wait days or weeks for the Pony Express to deliver the mail across the country, but today we receive e-mail from across the world almost instantly. Sure, there are those who clamor for the good old days when life was simpler, but, like it or not, technological change is a part of our world.

Beulah Henry's words still ring true, and they emphasize what this chapter is about: necessity and resourcefulness. In Chapter 1, we discussed the necessity of paying taxes to enable our society to function. In this chapter we'll talk about being resourceful by using technology to help you develop your tax plan and achieve the results you want.

Why Do It the e-Way?

The information revolution that has put a computer on almost every desk and lap has also developed a wide variety of applications that help make hard things easy and easy things even easier and faster. If that isn't enough, the personal computer has also made the Internet accessible to just about everyone.

The information revolution has also come to the world of taxes. While some people think this benefits only the "do-it-yourselfer," we think you'll find that there is something for every taxpayer. There are options for those who want to do it themselves, as well as for those who would prefer to have nothing to do with it at all. We're going to explore a variety of tax-related tasks from preparing a return to obtaining live help via the Internet, and we'll do it by focusing on the **e-way**

The Joys of e-Filing

In Chapter 10, we discussed different ways to file your tax return, one of which was e-filing. Remember, e-filing refers only to how you file (send) your return with the IRS, not to the method you or your tax professional used to prepare it. Because it is such an important topic, we want to spend a little more time on it.

According to the IRS, e-filing is the fastest and most accurate method of filing your tax return. Why? Because it's convenient and removes the chance that your tax return will be lost or delayed in the mail. Once your tax return has been e-filed, the IRS will send a notification, within forty-eight hours, that they have indeed received and accepted your return. You don't get that at the post office!

The IRS's computers will automatically check your e-filed return for errors and missing information—a more accurate method for processing returns (the IRS reports an error rate of less that 1 percent). If you owe, you can e-file early and pay later (on or before April 15), but if you're getting a refund, e-filing halves the time it takes to process a paper return. If you e-file and choose direct deposit, the time shrinks to as little as ten days.

As you can see, there are numerous benefits to e-filing your tax return. If you haven't already, give it a try. We think you'll like it.

plain talk

Doing it the e-way means performing a task electronically, such as with a personal computer, telephone, or with the Internet.

What's Right for You?

When it comes to preparing and filing your tax return, you have many electronic options. Choices include preparing and filing your tax return yourself using either a personal computer with tax preparation software or an online service. If you choose one of these options, you can also choose to send your self-prepared return to a tax professional to check your work. Another option is to have an online tax professional prepare and file your return for you. If you have a tax question that you'd like to ask a tax professional, there's an electronic option for that, too.

One note before we go into detail: We will present each electronic option in terms of what it has to offer without naming specific products or providers. Be aware that there are major differences in providers of software and online products and services. You need to do your homework and only do business with reputable companies that can provide you with high-quality products and services that are safe and secure. Price is always a consideration, but don't be penny-wise and pound-foolish. Your taxes are much too important for that.

Tax Preparation Software

One of the first electronic options for preparing and filing an income tax return was the development of **tax preparation software** for your personal computer. These programs assist do-it-yourselfers with preparing and filing their returns.

Instead of you doing all the manual labor, these programs do it for you—no more pencils and calculators. Instead, the user is led through the preparation process and prompted for information at each step. Along the way, some programs provide advice to uncover deductions or credits that might have been missed and tips and advice for the future. Others assist the user in making tax-wise investments, such as using a refund to fund an IRA.

No matter how intelligent the program may be, your tax return will turn out only as accurate and complete as the information you enter. It's advantageous to be savvy enough to sort through the questions and advice that may be presented to better understand what is being recommended.

Should you consider using a personal computer and tax preparation software? You may want to consider this option if any of the following apply to you:

- **You're a do-it-yourselfer, you are confident in your abilities, and you want to prepare and file your own tax return**
- **You prefer to store your tax-related information on your own computer** (as opposed to online or with a tax professional)
- **You need to file multiple returns, such as for family members or in multiple states**
- **You prefer an electronic option, but have a slow or unreliable Internet connection**

When choosing tax preparation software, determine what your needs are and how well the program can meet them. Depending on the answer, you may choose from programs that offer only basic federal income tax return preparation to deluxe programs that offer much more, including state income tax return preparation, integrated advice, and planning features, just to name a few. Remember, not all software is created equal. Find a program from a reliable and reputable source that best fits your needs.

fast fact

When you e-file your return and choose direct deposit, you'll get your refund in as few as ten days.

Online Tax Preparation

Tax preparation, like many other activities, has made the move to the Internet. Online tax programs have features similar to that of tax preparation software, but there are a number of differences. Two key differences are where the program is located and where your data is stored. With **online tax preparation**, there is no program to install on your computer: the program is located and run on the provider's server and accessed from its Web site via the Internet. Likewise, your data is not stored on your computer, but on the provider's server.

Is it safe? As with any other service provided via the Web, the answer to that depends on your provider. Look for a provider that secures both your tax return and your payment information. Most providers will promote their security measures up front, but here's another quick check you can do. Look at the URL (Uniform Resource Locator, an address on the Internet) in the address window of your web browser. It should start out with "https:" The important part is the "s," which indicates that you are on a secure site. Another quick check is to look for a closed padlock at the bottom of your browser. That also indicates that you are on a secure site. If the site is not secure, there is a chance someone else may be able to see your data.

Who should consider using online tax preparation? You may want to consider this option if:

- **You're a do-it-yourselfer, you are confident in your abilities, and you want to prepare and file your own tax return**
- **You don't have a computer of your own, or you don't want your data to be stored on the personal computer that is used to prepare and file your return**
- **You don't want to install any software on a personal computer before using the program**

plain talk

Using online tax preparation is a method of preparing your tax return via the Internet. The program is stored and run on the provider's server.

Online tax preparation sites allow you to complete your tax return anywhere you have access to the Internet. You can start preparing your return from one computer and finish it from another, since the program and your data are not stored on the computer.

✓─────────────────────────────➤ **Software and Online Tax Preparation Checklist**

Use this list to compare options and decide what is right for you.

☐ **Advice**—If you need advice on a tax issue, can you get it from a live person? We'll talk more about advice later in the chapter.

☐ **Customizable to your situation**—Does the program ask you only the questions that relate to your tax situation, thus saving you time?

☐ **Data organization**—Some programs have a feature that helps you organize your data before you get started. Think of it as a virtual shoebox.

☐ **Double-check**—Does the program check your return and point out missing information and missed opportunities for deductions? Does it flag entries that might be questioned by the IRS?

☐ **Filing options**—The program should give you the option to e-file or to print ready-to-file forms.

☐ **Form selection and automatic calculation**—Does the program automatically select the forms you will need and perform the calculations?

☐ **Forms and schedules**—Depending on your tax situation, you may need additional forms or schedules to complete your return, such as Schedule C if you're self-employed. Are they available in the software or can you go to the provider's Web site to download them?

☐ **Free trial**—Some online tax preparation providers allow you to enter your data in your return before purchasing the service. This gives you a chance to decide if online tax preparation is the right option for you. Take a test drive and kick the virtual tires to make sure the program meets your needs. Software offers a similar option, but you must purchase the software to try it, and if you don't like it, you must return the software to get your money back.

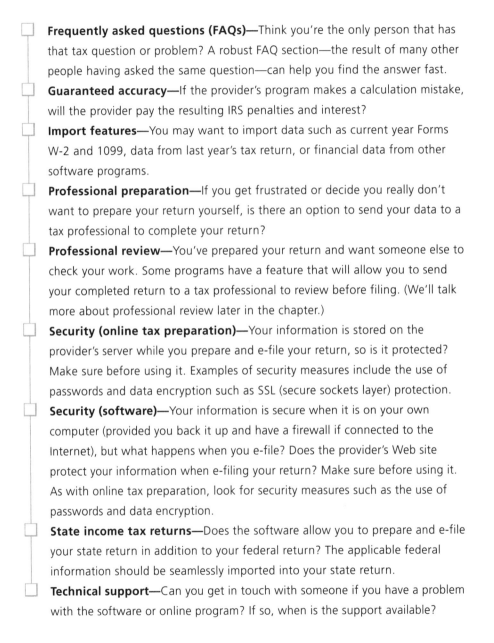
☐ **Frequently asked questions (FAQs)**—Think you're the only person that has that tax question or problem? A robust FAQ section—the result of many other people having asked the same question—can help you find the answer fast.

☐ **Guaranteed accuracy**—If the provider's program makes a calculation mistake, will the provider pay the resulting IRS penalties and interest?

☐ **Import features**—You may want to import data such as current year Forms W-2 and 1099, data from last year's tax return, or financial data from other software programs.

☐ **Professional preparation**—If you get frustrated or decide you really don't want to prepare your return yourself, is there an option to send your data to a tax professional to complete your return?

☐ **Professional review**—You've prepared your return and want someone else to check your work. Some programs have a feature that will allow you to send your completed return to a tax professional to review before filing. (We'll talk more about professional review later in the chapter.)

☐ **Security (online tax preparation)**—Your information is stored on the provider's server while you prepare and e-file your return, so is it protected? Make sure before using it. Examples of security measures include the use of passwords and data encryption such as SSL (secure sockets layer) protection.

☐ **Security (software)**—Your information is secure when it is on your own computer (provided you back it up and have a firewall if connected to the Internet), but what happens when you e-file? Does the provider's Web site protect your information when e-filing your return? Make sure before using it. As with online tax preparation, look for security measures such as the use of passwords and data encryption.

☐ **State income tax returns**—Does the software allow you to prepare and e-file your state return in addition to your federal return? The applicable federal information should be seamlessly imported into your state return.

☐ **Technical support**—Can you get in touch with someone if you have a problem with the software or online program? If so, when is the support available?

Professional Review

Once you decide which software or online preparation option is best for you, you can prepare your tax return for e-filing or printing. But perhaps you are a little anxious. Did you take every available deduction or credit to which you were entitled? Did you make a mistake and deduct something you shouldn't have? Maybe you just want someone to take a look and give you a little peace of mind that everything you did is correct.

Some software and online providers offer professional review as a feature that you can add to the program you have chosen. After you prepare your return, but before you file it, you send it electronically to a tax professional for review. The tax professional checks it over, gives you some feedback, and answers specific questions before you file your return. This usually costs extra, but it offers you some reassurance. Often, the tax professional who reviews your return also provides assistance and representation in case of an IRS audit.

smart step

Before sending your tax or financial information over the Internet, make sure the data is secure and can be viewed only by those you intend to see it.

All software and online tax applications are not created equal, and the same is true for professional review. Find a reputable provider that can supply you with a competent and qualified tax professional to review your return. And always make sure that your information is secure before you send it to anyone to review.

Online Professional Tax Service

Is there an option that would let you take advantage of the convenience of online preparation with the security of having a tax professional complete and e-file your return? You bet! Think of it as traditional goes new wave, East meets West, boy meets girl, a marriage made in . . . cyberspace.

This preparation option combines the best features of both worlds. You complete an online tax organizer that contains all the information needed to complete your return at your own pace, without loading any software, and from wherever you happen to have Internet access—at home, on the road, it's up to you. Then you send the file to your tax professional (a real live person) via the Internet, and he or she prepares and files your return for you. When your tax professional prepares your return, he or she will contact you (usually the e-way via a secure message board) if additional information is needed. You'll have a chance to ask questions and review your return before it is filed. It's like visiting a tax professional at the office, except it's an office on the Internet.

Who should consider using an online professional tax service? You may want to consider this option if you want the security of knowing that a tax professional prepared and filed your tax return. Online tax professionals function just like traditional tax professionals. They can handle complex tax returns and difficult tax situations, and they should guarantee their work. Since they operate via the Internet, an online tax pro may offer better schedule flexibility. Maybe your schedule doesn't make an office visit convenient, or maybe you want to work on completing your tax organizer at your own pace wherever you happen to be, or maybe you just want to have your tax return prepared while you're in your pajamas. This option makes it all possible.

Of course, not all online tax professionals are the same. Make sure you know who will be preparing your tax return. You may not know his or her name right away, but you should know who the professional works for and the individual's qualifications. Find a reputable provider that can supply you with a competent and qualified tax professional to prepare and file your return. As is with every other online option we have discussed, always make sure that your information is secure before you send it to anyone.

THE CHALLENGE

Steve is a tech-savvy guy. He loves surfing the Web via his high-speed Internet connection, finding cool gaming sites, and downloading music and applications to his personal computer. His motto is, "Do it the e-way or hit the freeway." When it came time to prepare and file his tax return, Steve knew the only option he wanted to pursue was to prepare and file using his personal computer. Steve went online, researched all the various providers and what they had to offer, and chose a reputable and reliable site to prepare his tax return online. Steve liked the convenience and the speed with which he received his refund because he also chose to e-file his return. A few years later Steve married, purchased a house, and started his own business. "When I saw all of the things that had changed this year and how complicated my life had become, I was concerned that I might miss something on my tax return," said Steve. "Quite frankly, with my new business, I just don't have the time to do it myself anymore." Steve needed some options.

THE PLAN

Steve knew a traditional tax professional would prepare and file his tax return, but because he was working long hours, he didn't feel he had the time to go to an appointment. So he reached for the tool with which he was most comfortable—the Internet—to research his options. "Instead of going to a tax professional, I wanted him to come to me," said Steve. He chose an online tax professional to prepare and e-file his return. "My tax professional prepared my return, reviewed it with me, answered all of my questions, and then e-filed it for me, and I never left the house. As a matter of fact, I never even bothered to change out of my shorts," Steve added. "It's still do it the e-way or hit the freeway for me."

Tax Questions—Who Ya Gonna Call?

smart step

Make sure your communications over the Internet are secure. Avoid sending personal or confidential information via standard e-mail.

No matter how you choose to have your tax return prepared and filed, you may have a tax-related question that you need to ask. If you already have a tax professional, give him or her a call. If you don't have a tax professional, have already looked at the FAQs in your software or online preparation program, and if you still have questions, whom should you ask? A co-worker, a relative, or your neighbor over the back fence? All of these people may have good intentions, but you probably don't want to rely on them for tax advice. Let's face it, the tax code is complicated and changes often. Inaccurate advice can cost you money and get you in hot water with the IRS. Fortunately, there is an e-way to get your questions answered by a representative of the IRS or a qualified tax professional.

The IRS offers a few different options to get your questions answered via the Web or by telephone. The IRS Web site—www.irs.gov—has an FAQ section that you can search either by category or by keyword. The site provides many valuable resources, including publications, forms, and other tools, so it may take some time to familiarize yourself with it and surf your way through. If you can't find an answer there, you can always give the IRS a call at 1-800-829-1040 and talk to a live representative.

If you prefer not to ask the IRS for advice, you can contact a tax professional by telephone, online chat, or e-mail. Every situation is different, and a tax professional will respond with advice that is tailored to fit your situation.

Here's some advice on getting advice. We've said it before, but it bears repeating: Be sure you know who is behind the scenes providing online tax advice. The advice you receive will only be as good as the advisor providing it. Some providers utilize tax advisors who are certified professionals and whose advice is guaranteed, while other providers use advisors who are not certified and their advice is not guaranteed.

If you receive advice via e-mail, look for a provider that uses a secure message board for you to post questions and receive answers. Message boards are similar to e-mail, although you won't use your e-mail program to send and receive messages. Before choosing this option, check out the provider thoroughly to determine if it's using e-mail or a message board. The term e-mail is often used generically to describe communications back and forth across the Web.

Other Online Resources

Anyone can put up a Web site and then sell just about anything, say just about anything, and dispense whatever advice they see fit. But don't think that everything you see on the Internet must be taken with a grain of salt. In addition to the IRS Web site at www.irs.gov, there are other reliable and reputable Web sites that provide valuable tools and resources to assist in the development and implementation of your tax plan. These online resources will not only help you get your tax planning started, they'll also guide you to answers to your tax-related questions.

Web sites can offer a variety of tax-related resources, including calculators, fast facts, tax planning tips, downloadable tax forms, and even advice. Some will even invite you to sign up to receive periodic e-mails regarding changes in tax law. All of these features can make your tax planning easier and help you become more tax-savvy.

smart step

When visiting Web sites, always read and understand their privacy policies. It is important to know how your personal data will be used.

Check out some tools that are available online to assist you:

- **e-File status**—Check with the IRS on the status of your refund if you e-file.
- **Home mortgage calculator**—Use this tool to see how much you can save in taxes with your qualified home mortgage.
- **Income tax courses**—Do you want to know even more about taxes? Enroll online in an income tax course to increase your knowledge.
- **Tax outlook calculator**—Use this tool to project how you will be affected in the future by recent tax law changes.
- **What's right for me?**—This interactive feature, available on certain Web sites, helps you to determine your best options for preparing and filing your return.
- **Withholding calculator**—Are you withholding enough from each paycheck? Find out.

And many more.

Should You Pass on the e-Way and Use a Traditional Tax Professional?

We have reviewed a number of online and software options, but you still might be unsure whether the e-way is the right choice for you. Perhaps your tax situation has changed dramatically (did you purchase a home or get married?). Maybe you're self-employed and have a complicated return. Maybe you don't want to prepare your own return. As we said before, we think utilizing a tax professional is a smart idea. A traditional tax professional will help you prepare and file your return and give you plenty of tax-wise advice along the way.

the ESSENTIALS

1 Many electronic resources are available to help you develop and implement your tax plan, including a variety of software and online options. Choose the option that works for you.

2 The key differences between preparing your tax return online or with a personal computer and software are where the preparation program is located and run and where your information is stored.

3 Online professional tax service combines the security of having a tax professional prepare and e-file your return with the convenience of the Internet.

4 Before sending your tax or financial information over the Internet, make sure the data is secure and can be viewed only by those you intend to see it.

5 Not all software and online providers are equal. Choose only those that are both reliable and reputable.

13 [TAXING MATTERS: Frequently Asked Tax Questions and Answers]

"A prudent question is one-half of wisdom."
—Francis Bacon

With hundreds of thousands of tax rules and provisions embedded in the IRS tax code, it's tough to cover everything in just one book. To this point, we've focused on the tax strategies you'll use the most—exemptions, deductions, credits, investments, and college planning, just to name a few—but we want to give you information on other tax issues as well.

Following are commonly asked questions, organized alphabetically, on other important tax planning areas, from adoption to charitable giving, to Social Security and more.

Adoption

Q. **My husband and I are completing an international adoption. Have there been any changes to the adoption tax credit?**

A. There have been several changes. The credit is now permanent. For expenses paid after 2001, the credit limit was increased to $10,000 per eligible child and the income level at which the credit begins to be phased out has been increased. For international adoptions, you claim the credit in the year the adoption is completed. For more information regarding your specific situation, talk to a tax professional.

Q. **My wife and I are confused about claiming the credit for our adoption expenses. What do we claim and when?**

A. If you adopt a United States citizen or resident, claim the credit for the year *following* the year in which you paid the expenses. However, if the adoption becomes final during the year in which you pay the expenses, take the credit in that year. Note that when attempting to adopt a United States citizen or resident, you receive the credit even if the adoption falls through.

If you adopt a child who isn't a citizen or resident, you may claim your credit *only* in the year the adoption becomes final. Unfortunately, if the adoption falls through, you can't claim the credit at all.

In either case, qualified expenses you pay in years after the adoption is finalized are claimed as a credit in the year paid.

Alimony

Q. **Can I treat a divorced spouse as a dependent instead of taking the deduction for alimony paid? If so, can I write off her deductible expenses? Her only income was the alimony.**

A. You can't claim your ex-spouse as your dependent, and you can't deduct any of her expenses. You can take an above-the-line deduction for qualified alimony you paid.

Q. **Can spousal support be deducted?**

A. If payments are to be considered alimony, and therefore deductible, all of the following must be true:

1. The payments are required by a divorce decree or written separation instrument
2. The payer and recipient do not file a joint return
3. The payments are in cash, which includes checks or money orders
4. The payments are not designated in the separation or divorce instrument as *not* alimony
5. Spouses are legally separated under a decree of divorce or separation and are not members of the same household
6. Payments are not required after the death of the recipient's spouse
7. Payments are not designated as child support

Alimony payments are deductible by the payer and includible in the income of the recipient.

Bankruptcy

Q. **I declared bankruptcy this year. Will my bankruptcy affect my tax return?**

A. Yes. Just how depends on a variety of factors, including the type of bankruptcy. This is one of those situations in which it is smart to visit a tax professional.

Benefits

Q. **Are health insurance premiums tax-deductible if they are taken out of my paycheck as pre-tax dollars?**

A. No, they aren't deductible. However, having the premiums taken out pre-tax is a greater benefit because they reduce your adjusted gross income, which may, in turn, increase some other tax benefits.

Q. **Can I deduct COBRA payments? If so, what form should I use?**

A. Your payments will be deductible as a medical expense on Schedule A. Your total qualified medical expenses are deductible to the extent they exceed 7.5 percent of your AGI.

Charity

Q. **I volunteer for a variety of charities and incur out-of-pocket expenses while doing so. Are these expenses deductible?**

A. You may deduct (as an itemized deduction on Schedule A) unreimbursed out-of-pocket expenses that are directly attributable to services you render to charitable organizations. Examples of such expenses include the cost of postage, stationery, telephone calls, craft supplies, equipment, and food you provide while performing duties for a qualified organization. If you use your car while providing charitable services, you may deduct 14 cents per mile (for 2002) or the cost of gas and oil. In addition, parking fees and tolls are deductible regardless of whether you use the standard mileage rate or the cost of gas and oil. You may also deduct the cost of travel, meals, and lodging you incur while performing services away from home, provided the trip is for charity and not a disguised vacation.

Q. **Our church raffled off a new car as part of a fund-raising drive. Are prizes awarded by churches tax-free?**

A. The fair market value of the car (reduced by the cost of the winning ticket) is taxable income to the winner. He or she can deduct as an itemized deduction what they paid for the other raffle tickets.

Children

Q. **What tax breaks can I get for the expenses I pay for care of my child while I work?**

A. Assuming your child is under age thirteen or incapable of self-care, you may claim a credit for a portion of your child-care expenses on Form 2441. But here's another idea. If your employer has a child-care benefit program, the tax savings may be larger than those for the credit. Check out this option with your employer, and then ask your tax professional to estimate your tax savings both ways.

Q. **The money I pay my ex-wife for child support is used mostly for day care. Am I eligible for the child-care credit?**

A. Unfortunately, you aren't eligible for the credit because your ex-wife has custody of the children.

Divorce

Q. **Can I deduct the legal fees from my divorce?**

A. Legal fees connected with getting a divorce are not deductible, except to the extent of any tax advice-related fees specifically itemized on a statement from your lawyer. Such fees are deducted as a tax preparation fee on Schedule A.

Foreign Issues

Q. **I began working outside of the United States in October, and I will be out of the country indefinitely. What are the laws on income earned abroad?**

A. You must continue to file your United States tax return, reporting all income. Because you are living and working out of the country, you may qualify to claim an exclusion of earned income (up to $80,000 for 2002) plus excess living costs. Because you were not out of the country for the entire year, the maximum exclusion will be prorated. Note, however, that if your pay is from the government as its employee, you don't qualify for the exclusion.

Q. **My Form 1099-DIV from my mutual fund has an entry for foreign tax paid. How does this entry affect my tax return?**

A. You can claim a credit for the foreign tax paid. If the total foreign tax you paid exceeds $300 for the year ($600 if you file jointly with your spouse), you must complete Form 1116. Otherwise, you can usually enter the foreign tax paid directly on Form 1040.

Gambling

Q. **Can I use cash withdrawal receipts from a casino ATM to prove that I had a gambling loss?**

A. No, the IRS does not consider ATM withdrawal receipts proof of your gambling losses. The best record you can provide is a written log of your gambling activity, including where and how much you won and lost.

Homes

Q. **On the closing statement for my principal residence, some of my costs are identified as points. Are points currently deductible?**

A. If the points represent fees that you paid solely for the use of money, they may be deductible as qualified residence interest in the year paid. A fee that you pay as a specific service charge in connection with a loan is a charge for services rendered and is not deductible as interest. Here are the criteria for the points to be deductible in full in the current year:

1. The underlying loan has to be for the purchase or improvement of, and secured by, your principal residence.
2. The charging of points must be an established business practice in your area and the points you pay must not be in excess of the usual amount charged in your area.
3. The amount is computed as a percentage of the stated principal amount of the mortgage.
4. You must pay at closing an amount at least equal to the points charged. Money for this payment must come from a source other than the lender.
5. The points must clearly be shown on the settlement statement.

However, before you automatically deduct the points all at once, check with your tax professional to determine if electing to deduct the points over the life of the loan is a better option.

Q. **My wife and I recently sold our main home. How can we avoid paying a large amount in taxes?**

A. If:

- **Both you and your wife lived in the home for at least two of the five years immediately preceding the date of sale**
- **During that five-year period, either of you owned the home for at least two years**
- **Neither of you have sold another home within the past two years**
- **You file jointly**

you can exclude from tax (meaning you will pay no tax on) up to $500,000 of gain. The maximum exclusion amount is $250,000 for taxpayers not filing a joint return. You'll pay tax on any gain in excess of your maximum exclusion amount, usually at the capital gains rate of 20 percent. If you were in the home less than two years, the taxable gain may or may not be prorated, depending on your circumstances.

Q. **I've heard there's a tax break for IRA money used to buy a home. Is that true?**

A. Yes. You can withdraw up to $10,000 from a traditional or Roth IRA, and, if you use the money to buy a first home, the money so used isn't subject to the 10 percent penalty on early distributions. Taxable income from the distribution is determined under the usual rules. The money may be used to purchase a first home for you,

your spouse, your children or grandchildren, your parents, or even your grandparents.

A "first-time home buyer," for this purpose, is generally a person who had no ownership interest in a home during the two-year period ending on the date the money is used to buy the home. There are some other technical, but important, provisions concerning using IRA funds to purchase a first home, so check with your tax professional *before* you take any money from an IRA.

Marriage

Q. **My wife and I are married, employed, and filing jointly. How do I avoid having to pay more money when we file our return?**

A. The key for both of you is having enough taxes withheld to prevent an unpleasant surprise at tax time. Careful completion of Form W-4, with its accompanying worksheets, will allow you to come near breaking even at tax time, or you can tailor your withholding to assure yourself a refund of a size you choose. The procedures are sometimes complicated. Your tax professional can customize your Form W-4 to fit your needs.

Q. **My wife and I both work, and we file jointly. She is behind in her federally insured student loan payments, and we understand that the government**

will keep our refund in partial payment of the debt. I think that's fair enough for her part of the refund, but not for mine. Is there anything I can do?

A. In tax terminology, you're called an injured spouse. To receive your share of the refund, file Form 8379, Injured Spouse Claim and Allocation.

Q. My husband and I were recently married. Do we have to file jointly this year?

A. Even if you were married late in the year, you are considered married for the entire year. That means you must choose between filing jointly or using the married filing separately status. Generally, filing jointly is the wise decision.

Q. When is it an advantage for a married couple to file separately rather than jointly?

A. Filing separately is not often advantageous. But, depending on how your income and deductions are divided—for example, if the lower-income spouse has a significant amount of medical expenses or employee business expenses—it may be advantageous. Be aware that filing separately may cause the loss of some benefits. For example, you can't generally claim the earned income credit or the child-care credit on separate returns.

Medical Expenses

Q. My five-year-old daughter needed to undergo some specialized medical tests at a hospital two hundred miles from our home. I drove her to the hospital and stayed for two nights in a motel. I know my daughter's hospital expenses are deductible, but are my travel expenses?

A. Because your daughter was unable to travel alone, you may deduct your travel expenses, including a mileage allowance for your transportation and up to $50 per night for lodging. If your daughter stayed with you in the motel rather than at the hospital, you could deduct up to $100 per night because each of you has a separate $50-per-night limit. However, you may not deduct your meal expenses in this situation.

Q. I did not list some medical deductions on my 2001 return. Can I claim these expenses on my 2002 return?

A. No, you cannot. You need to file an amended return for the prior year to add those deductions.

Q. I have unreimbursed medical bills in the amount of $3,000. Can I deduct these expenses on my federal tax return?

A. Most medical expenses and expenses for prescription medication and insulin can be claimed as an itemized deduction to the extent they exceed 7.5 percent of your adjusted gross income.

Q. **I recently quit smoking with the help of an intensive program offered at a local hospital. I also got help from nicotine gum I purchased over the counter. Can I deduct my costs as a medical expense if I itemize?**

A. The cost of the hospital-sponsored program is deductible, but the cost of non-prescription aids such as nicotine gum or patches is not.

Q. **My doctor told me my high blood pressure is related to the excess weight I admit I carry. She told me to enroll in a weight-loss program. Is the cost of the program tax-deductible?**

A. Yes. Because you enrolled in the program as part of the treatment for your high blood pressure, you can add the cost of the weight-loss program to your other medical expenses. You can also deduct the cost of attending periodic meetings, but *not* the cost of any diet food you buy that is a substitute for the food you normally eat.

Q. **What is an Archer MSA?**

A. An Archer MSA (Medical Savings Account) is an account set up exclusively for paying the qualified medical expenses of the account holder, spouse, and dependent(s) in conjunction with an HDHP (high-deductible health plan). To be eligible for an MSA, you must be an employee of a small employer (who has an average of 50 or fewer employees) or self-employed. You must also have a high-deductible health plan, have no other health insurance coverage except permitted coverage, and meet other requirements.

Military

Q. **My husband is in the military, stationed outside his state of residency, and I'm a resident of the state in which he is serving on active duty. Is it possible to file our federal tax return as married filing jointly but file our state tax return as married filing separate?**

A. It depends. Some states require that you use the same filing status on both the state and federal income tax returns, but some states allow you to file differently. A tax professional can explain the rules that apply to your particular situation.

Q. **How does my military service in a combat zone affect my tax liability?**

A. As a member of the Armed Forces serving in a combat zone (currently, the Kosovo area, the Persian Gulf, the former Yugoslavia hazardous duty area, and Afghanistan), you get a number of tax breaks. Some examples are:

1. An interest-free extension of the deadlines to file your return, pay federal income taxes, make an IRA contribution, and take certain other actions. This extension lasts for the period you are in the combat zone plus (typically) one hundred eighty days. The extension of deadlines covers both you and your spouse, regardless of whether you file a joint return or separate returns. The extension also applies to civilians serving in a combat zone as support for the U.S. Armed Forces, such as Red Cross workers, accredited correspondents, and civilian personnel acting under the direction of the U.S. Armed Forces.

2. For members of the U.S. Armed Forces who are on active duty in a combat zone, military pay is excluded from federal income tax, in full for enlisted personnel and partially for officers. The excludable income will not be included in taxable wages on your Form W-2.

3. Most states follow the federal rule for enlisted personnel and some exempt all combat pay for officers.

Q. Do active duty military personnel receive any other tax breaks or unique tax opportunities?

A. Military employees do receive special benefits, including exclusion of their subsistence and quarters allowance and other nontaxable benefits, as shown on their leave and earnings statement. Military personnel are residents of the state listed as their home of record, so no other state can tax their military compensation. For additional information about taxation of military personnel, see IRS Publication 3 or consult a tax professional.

Social Security

Q. Next year I will retire and start drawing Social Security. I want to take a part-time job to keep busy, but I don't want to jeopardize my Social Security benefits. How much money can I earn before I start losing benefits?

A. If you're sixty-five or older, you can earn an unlimited amount without having to pay back any of your Social Security benefits. If you're under sixty-five, you may have to repay some of your benefits if you earn more than $11,280 for 2002 ($11,520 for 2003). The Social Security Administration announces the figure for the upcoming year in October of each year. This information is also available by calling 1-800-772-1213.

Q. I'm single and will be receiving Social Security benefits for the first time in 2002. Will I have to pay taxes on these benefits?

A. Generally, if your other income plus half your Social Security benefits plus tax–exempt interest is $25,000 or less, none of your benefits are taxable. In no case will more than 85 percent of your benefits be taxable. Complete the worksheet in the Form 1040 or Form 1040A instructions to determine the taxable amount.

Tax Due Payments

Q. I had a balance due and had to pay $1,964 when I filed my federal tax return last year. Can I deduct that on my return this year?

A. No. Federal income tax balances due aren't deductible and refunds aren't taxable.

Q. If on April 15, I mail a check for the tax due in full along with an explanation, but I mail my actual tax forms a few days later, will that protect me against any fines?

A. If you choose to make only a payment on April 15, do not submit it by itself. Include Form 4868 with your check. That will prevent you from being penalized and will provide you with extra time to prepare your return.

Q. I could not pay taxes for several years because of a financial hardship. Now I want to come clean. Is leniency allowed because I simply could not afford to pay for several years?

A. First, you need to contact a tax professional for assistance. Second, you need to file your returns as quickly as possible. If you're now able to pay what you owe, do so quickly. If not, you may be able to arrange installment payments. You might even get the IRS to accept an offer-in-compromise, meaning the IRS would accept less than the full amount. The offer-in-compromise may be ac-cepted if you can show you cannot currently and will not in the future be able to pay your taxes.

Tax Liability

Q. I just found out today that my paychecks are going to be garnished for the next seven months. How do I report this on my tax return?

A. The income is still taxable. If the garnished wages are for alimony payments, you will have a deduction. But if the garnished wages are for child support, there is no deduction.

Q. I am a single person with no dependents. I am interested in minimizing my taxes. I have no stocks or other investments. How do I successfully minimize my taxes?

A. To reduce your tax liabilities, you can:

- **Contribute to a traditional IRA, if you qualify to make deductible payments**
- **Purchase a home**
- **Increase your charitable contributions**
- **Invest in tax-exempt investments**
- **Invest in a tax-deferred retirement plan if your employer offers one**

These are just a few ideas. You may want to consult a tax professional and financial advisor to take advantage of these and other options.

Now, Get Ready to Make the Most of Your Tax Situation

Congratulations! You've finished reading the **H&R Block Tax Planning Advisor**. You should now know a great deal more about taxes than you did before you started.

Now it's time to put some of the tax-planning strategies discussed in this book to good use. You can begin your new tax-planning program by taking the fundamentals you learned in these pages and applying them to your personal tax situation.

Remember, tax planning doesn't have to be entirely your burden. Call a tax professional for some of the tougher tax issues you face and gain even more benefits in the process.

Whether you're hiring a professional or going it alone, remember one last thing: Taxes are indeed what we pay for a civilized society, but in the end it's your money. You earned it, and you have the right, as spelled out in the tax code, to take steps to keep more of it for you and your family.

With this book, hopefully you've learned how to do just that. Happy tax planning.

resources

When choosing your resources for tax advice, make sure they are reliable and reputable. Here are some resources you may want to consider.

Internal Revenue Service

The IRS provides a variety of resource material including forms, publications, advice, and some tax-related tools available by mail, telephone, or online.

- **Live telephone assistance: 1-800-829-1040**
- **Live telephone assistance for people with a hearing impairment: 1-800-829-4059 (TDD)**
- **Tele-Tax recorded tax information: 1-800-829-4477**
- **Taxpayer advocate service: 1-877-777-4778**
- **Order forms or publications for delivery:**
  —via fax-on-demand: 1-703-368-9694
  —via U.S. Postal Service: 1-800-TAX-FORM (1-800-829-3676)
- **On the Web: www.irs.gov**

H&R Block

A trusted name in providing professional tax preparation and advice, H&R Block has a wide selection of available resources. These include tax return preparation and filing options, forms, advice, planning tools, tax preparation courses, and much more. In addition to its well known professional tax services, H&R Block provides a wide range of financial products and services. These include investment services and securities products, and a full range of home mortgage products.

To find out more:

- **Automated information line: 1-800-HRBLOCK (1-800-472-5625)**
- **On the Web: www.hrblock.com**
- **In-person: Visit one of more than 10,000 retail locations conveniently located near you. Visit www.hrblock.com to find the office nearest you.**

index

H&R Block, Inc. (www.hrblock.com) is a diversified company with subsidiaries that deliver tax services and financial advice, investment and mortgage products and services, and business accounting and consulting services.

As the world's largest tax services company, H&R Block served nearly 23 million clients during fiscal year 2002. Clients were served at H&R Block's approximately 10,400 retail offices worldwide, through its award-winning software, TaxCut®, and through its online tax services.

Investment services and securities products are offered through H&R Block Financial Advisors Inc., member NYSE, SIPC. H&R Block Inc. and H&R Block Services, Inc. are not registered broker-dealers. H&R Block Mortgage Corp. offers retail mortgage products. Option One Mortgage Corp. offers wholesale mortgage products and a wide range of mortgage services. RSM McGladrey Inc. serves mid-sized businesses with accounting, tax and consulting services.

IT'S NOT THE COFFEE THAT'S GIVING YOU THE JITTERS.

Doing your own taxes can be pretty un-nerving. Leave it to the professionals to help you relax and get you every cent you have coming.

save
$10

Save $10.00 on income tax preparation

 H&R BLOCK®

TAKE THE "ING" OUT OF TAX.

Why struggle on your own? Let the professionals help. We understand the latest tax code changes and can make them work for you.

save $10

Save $10.00 on income tax preparation

 H&R BLOCK®

Code 810